Water, Water Everywhere . . .
Scottsdale Museum of Contemporary Art

This catalogue was published on the occasion of the exhibition *Water, Water Everywhere . . .*, organized by the Scottsdale Museum of Contemporary Art.

The exhibition has received major funding from The Andy Warhol Foundation for the Visual Arts, Inc., New York. Sponsored by Nargess and Ali Salass; SRP; Rebecca and Alexander Stewart; and the SMoCA Salon. Catalogue supported in part by SMoCA Docents.

Scottsdale Museum of Contemporary Art
May 14 – September 4, 2005

Published by
Scottsdale Museum of Contemporary Art
7380 East Second Street
Scottsdale, Arizona 85251

Design by
Scott Zukowski, Texas Studio, Los Angeles

Printed and bound by
C & C Offset Printing Co., China

Distributed by
Trucatriche
3800 Main Street, Suite 8
Chula Vista, CA 91911
Tel 619.426.2690
Fax 619.426.2695
info@trucatriche.com
www.trucatriche.com

Library of Congress Cataloging-in-Publication Data *Water, Water Everywhere . . .* / exhibition curated by Marilu Knode; essays by Marilu Knode and Weng Choy Lee

ISBN 0967026571
Library of Congress Control Number: 2005922028

The Scottsdale Cultural Council, a private, nonprofit 501(C)3-management organization, administers the arts and cultural affairs of the City of Scottsdale, Arizona, and manages SMoCA as well as the Scottsdale Center for the Performing Arts and the Scottsdale Public Art Program.

Supported by the Arizona Commission on the Arts with funding from the State of Arizona and the National Endowment for the Arts. Partial funding provided by Arizona ArtShare, the state arts endowment fund, through public and private contributions.

Water, Water Everywhere . . .

Scottsdale Museum of Contemporary Art

* * * * *

Marilu Knode

Lara Baladi
Dorothy Cross
Jacci Den Hartog
Stan Douglas
Tony Feher
Robert Gober
Laura Horelli
Roni Horn
Ange Leccia
Sabrina Mezzaqui
Rivane Neuenschwander
Jun Nguyen-Hatsushiba
Song Dong
Janaina Tschäpe
Carrie Yamaoka

Water is an image of impermanence. It is the ultimate metaphor for flux, a reminder that the state of meaning—like the state of matter—is fluid and transitory. An ordinary "rain" in Atlanta often pounds relentlessly from the sky, whereas the seasonal "monsoons" in Phoenix can amount to a few minutes of mere sprinkle. Water is universal; its significance, however, is geographically and culturally specific. In the mythology of ancient Rome, Neptune was a triumphant, sometimes wrathful old charioteer; in Yoruba mythology, Oshun is a sensuous but bashful river goddess with powers of divination. Amid the desert of Arizona, water travels to my faucet via a vast network of canals and emerges on demand, if laden with chemicals that are prone to leaving a crusty residue. The nearest lake has banks of concrete. We drink designer water from plastic bottles. "Water" is a very relative idea.

For artists, the subject of water provides a flexible lens that also serves to focus attention on the globalization of contemporary art practice today. The imagery of water speaks easily to peoples across borders, never failing to seduce viewers with its hypnotic, kinesthetic effects. The subject is so familiar, so very accessible, that it can harbor deep differences. Art historians struggle to define a model of globalism that is neither dominating nor universalist—a model that might enable a communal critical aesthetic discourse that does not subsume cultural and political distinctions. The subject of water, at once particular and general, is a convenient device for exploring the relationship of individual artistic identity to the international marketplace of experiences in the 21st century.

Water, Water Everywhere. . . is an ironic title for an exhibition presented in the desert in the middle of the summer. Its source—Samuel Taylor Coleridge's hallucinatory poem "The Rime of the Ancient Mariner"—may strike some as anachronistic: today, mention of mariners most likely brings to mind the professional baseball team. Yet irony, like poetry, begs contemplation. Consumed by daily concerns, most of us tend to dismiss the rubric of the epic journey to which the exhibition's title refers. What are the epic quests, the philosophical thirsts, of contemporary life? What helps us find our bearings, adrift in a sea of riches, in the age of information? How do we recognize today's albatrosses? How do we navigate global political storms and find dry land?

Many of the artists in *Water, Water Everywhere. . .* point to such psychological passages—tests of love, self-perception, nationhood and spiritual life. Collectively, they relocate the viewer's everyday microcosm of reality within a larger, worldly journey. These artists metaphorically ask the existential question that Coleridge's wise Hermit poses to his ancient Mariner, "What manner of man art thou?"

This exhibition is very much the result of Senior Curator Marilu Knode's long-standing commitment to internationalism. *Water, Water Everywhere. . .* is Marilu's first major show for the Scottsdale Museum of Contemporary Art and a wonderful manifestation of the energy and intelligence she brings to her position. Simultaneously conceptual and visceral, *Water, Water Everywhere. . .* proceeds from Marilu's belief that beauty and content are not mutually exclusive and may indeed swirl around each other. I am most grateful for her rigorous and expansive curatorial practice—and for the humor she brings to hard work.

This project furthers the Scottsdale Museum of Contemporary Art's mission to present programs of international scope and to enable the creation of new works by visiting artists, many of whom are thus introduced to the southwest. By doing so, we perpetuate the Museum's belief that art can be a catalyst—the object of an ongoing collective conversation that endures far beyond this wonderful mirage of water in the desert.

Introduction ~ Susan Krane, director

The idea of water as the subject of an exhibition came to me shortly after my arrival at the Scottsdale Museum of Contemporary Art. I had seen the work of Jun Nguyen-Hatsushiba in Tokyo several years ago, and his work called to mind a cascade of images by other artists with whom I had wanted to work, such as Tony Feher, Robert Gober and Janaina Tschäpe. With the unfailing support of director Susan Krane, who had the forbearance and faith to let me use one word—water—to inaugurate my contributions to the fulfillment of SMoCA's mission, the exhibition was born.

Every show I curate is built on the smart, lively, critical and seductive work of artists like those in *Water, Water Everywhere* . . . . I am inspired by my conversations with them, by their generosity of spirit and by their dedication to their dreams. My thanks go to Lara Baladi, Dorothy Cross, Jacci Den Hartog, Stan Douglas, Tony Feher, Robert Gober, Laura Horelli, Roni Horn, Ange Leccia, Sabrina Mezzaqui, Rivane Neuenschwander, Jun Nguyen-Hatsushiba, Song Dong, Janaina Tschäpe and Carrie Yamaoka for their support of this project.

The presentation is designed to bring together existing works with commissioned new pieces that allow artists to develop their oeuvre with a new audience in mind. Yona Bacher and Pamela Clapp at The Andy Warhol Foundation for the Visual Arts, Inc., New York, were instrumental in enabling SMoCA to achieve this goal. We were able to support new projects by Lara Baladi, Tony Feher and Song Dong. This gives our visitors a unique relationship to the artists, the art and its display, demonstrating SMoCA's commitment to encouraging artists in their development. We have also received great support from friends of the museum: Nargess and Ali Salass; Richard Hayslip, Manager, SRP; Rebecca and Alexander Stewart; and the SMoCA Salon. Ali and Nargess Salass were the first to pledge funds after they reviewed images of the show, and Ali graciously helped us fundraise. SMoCA thanks all of these important cultural leaders for their generous, ongoing support of contemporary art in Scottsdale.
I thank them all for their belief in the project and for their friendship.

Numerous galleries and collectors have been helpful in providing loans, interfacing with artists who are busy (and in remote locations), and providing much-needed support in the production of a complicated exhibition and catalogue. I'd like to thank the following: Linda Chinfen and Brodie Smith, Stan Douglas Studio, Vancouver; Angela Choon, David Zwirner Gallery, New York; Lucien Terras, D'Amelio Terras, New York; Darragh Hogan and Anne Kelly, Kerlin Gallery, Dublin; Adrian Turner and Victoria Cuthbert, Matthew Marks Gallery, New York; Claudia Carson, Robert Gober Studio, New York; Christopher Grimes, Christopher Grimes Gallery, Santa Monica; Barbara Weiss and Luise Essen, Galerie Barbara Weiss, Berlin; Thomas Dryll, Galerie Almine Rech, Paris; Verusca Piazzesi, galleria continua, San Gimignano, Italy; Kathryn Kanjo, ArtPace, San Antonio, Texas; Alexandre Gabriel and Daniele Dal Col, Galeria Fortes Vilaça, São Paulo; Jan Endlich, Lehmann Maupin Gallery, New York; Teka Selman, Brent Sikkema Gallery, New York; Heige Kim, Janaina Tschäpe Studio, New York; Nic Debs, Debs & Co., New York. Thanks also go to SMoCA graphic designer Wen-Hang Lin and student Wei-Meng Foo, who assisted Song Dong during his residency in Scottsdale.

I admire collectors who are willing to share objects of their private passion with the public. I am grateful to Rebecca and Alexander Stewart of Seattle, who continue to be inspiring friends and arts patrons; Linda Pace of San Antonio; Jones Day, Los Angeles; and private collectors in Scottsdale. Loans from these individuals make this project complete.

Special support and advice has come from Chris Mao and Danny Kreisberg of Chambers Fine Arts, New York. Chris has been instrumental in negotiations of the complex details of working with Song Dong. Our entire staff is grateful for his collaboration and goodwill.

Scott Zukowski, Texas Studio, Los Angeles, is a wonderful colleague who has designed an expressive and engaging catalogue. I thank him for his flexibility in the face of the exciting, sometimes frustrating, variables of the non-profit world. I am pleased to finally be working with Weng Choy Lee, whose smart, erudite and incisive readings of contemporary art and society are invigorating. Susan Krane, SMoCA director, provided critical insight and suggestions for my essay; I thank her for helping me make the clearest case for the importance of these artists and their works. Susan Martin, Abiqui, New Mexico, and Lucy Flint, Southborough, Massachusetts, lent their editorial skills to the catalogue. Special thanks to the SMoCA Docents (led by Alice Olsan) for their contribution to the publication. Pete Jones, designer, and partners Art Lundgren, Dave Duke and Brad Ghormely, of Catapult Design, Phoenix, attract audiences to our programs through their elegant invitation design.

Staff is always last to be thanked. We assume that since we are all paid, completing the tasks at hand is automatic. Working in a museum, one continually expects the unexpected. New challenges arise with every show. This project came together because of the dedication (and sometimes crafty) negotiations of our team.

Pat Evans and Bethe Myers kept this project moving along amid the whirlwind of the daily operations of the office; they are the pillars of the curatorial team. Neil Borowicz and Mike Goodwin pulled off the myriad installation details with aplomb and technical skill. Bill Thompson, our marketing and public relations guru, and Wen-Hang Lin, designer extraordinaire, helped shape the look of the presentation. Leo Tee and Michelle Kaps are ever-vigilant in producing events that match the ambitions of the exhibitions. Carolyn Robbins, Sally Lindsay, Elizabeth Cichanowicz, Elizabeth Theisen, Erin Kane and Cassandra Coblentz contribute to the success of all of SMoCA's programs. Frank Jacobson, President and CEO of the Scottsdale Cultural Council, which administers the arts and cultural affairs for the City of Scottsdale, is a steadfast supporter of SMoCA's activities and the challenging ideas and unique experiences they bring to our audience. I am continually thankful to my colleagues for their inventiveness and good cheer.

I won't talk about how water is a mirror, but it's hard to talk about water without talking about oneself.[1]

—Roni Horn

Marilu Knode

~ ~ ~ ~ ~ ~ ~ ~ ~ ~ ~ ~ ~ ~ ~ ~

Adapting Modernity

The works in *Water, Water Everywhere* . . . suggest the complex web of relationships between ideas, or things, that are cohesive or stable and those that are fluid or mobile. The tension between these two categories exists in the physical, social and moral spheres of the individual as well as in those of society at large. Despite the evidence that our world is predicated on flux, humans suffer from a deep psychological conflict between wanting a stable "I" and experiencing the impermanence of the ego.[2] Artists in *Water, Water Everywhere* . . . express this ambivalence through the metaphor of water in all of its varied forms, using video, photography, sculpture and painting to explore the meanings of our contemporary world. Water reconciles the states of change and stability: it is alternately liquid or solid, sometimes a bit of both. In its ubiquity and persistence through a multitude of cultural and religious traditions and fashions, it allows for the broadest possible range of projected meanings.

The artists in *Water, Water Everywhere* . . . are not the first to use this element symbolically in relation to large cultural concepts. Water has appeared in art to warn against political hubris and personal transgression and to represent the unknown—sexual experience, the unconscious and the mysteries of nature. Artists have represented myriad and conflicting traditions and myths involving water, from baptism and ablution to punitive deluge. Art, like water, is our mirror, reflecting what we see around us, what we want to be and what we hope to become.

Water's indispensability to human survival is testified to by its preeminence in religious and cultural myths around the globe.[3] These stories generally begin with the world existing as a mass of water until something—or someone—activates the differentiation of earth, sky and water. Carl Jung's "collective unconscious" returns us to this prehistoric era when humans—not yet marked by ethnic, racial and social distinctions—were fully embedded in the world. In contemporary Western societies, many instincts, practices and values go back to the ancient past, even when we are unaware of the connection. Although science has explained the natural world thoroughly enough to render the notion of an interceding god irrelevant, many humans still long for a deity. Science has not eradicated belief in the spirituality of nature, a touchstone of many ancient religious traditions around the world.

Some anthropologists believe that the historical roots of social discord can be found in the shift among people from cooperation to competition at the time when blood ties were supplanted by land ties. Earth became more valuable than blood, the water of life.[4] This deliberate alienation from what might be considered our innate inclination has given rise to tremendous suffering and displacement, for millennia. Much of the work in *Water,*

Water Everywhere . . . highlights the contrast between the integrity of ancient "blood ties" and the divisiveness of contemporary society and politics.

Given water's changeability, we ascribe to it a range of human behaviors and moods. We think of it as being soothing or destructive, comforting or frightening. By comparing water to ourselves we hope to understand it—and perhaps control it. Yet water escapes human boundaries, slipping over its riverbanks, flowing onshore uninvited, pouring torrentially from the sky unannounced.

"Water, water, everywhere / Nor any drop to drink" are lines from Samuel Taylor Coleridge's poem "The Rime of the Ancient Mariner," 1798.[5] The Mariner's ship sails off course toward the south, and is then becalmed. An albatross appears and becomes attached to the Mariner; it returns day after day, and eventually leads the ship northward toward more active air currents. The Mariner inexplicably shoots the bird. A terrible heat envelops the vessel, leading to the deaths of all on board save him. The spirits teach the Mariner a lesson—his dead shipmates rise to guide the ship back to shore. He is redeemed by expressing his love for all of God's creatures.

The phrase "water, water, everywhere" appears after the Mariner has shot the albatross. His act is emblematic of disregard for the spiritual dimension in nature; his murderous impulse shears him from the world around him. Coleridge's poem puts rhythm to the human destructiveness that normally comes out in staccato bursts of fire. That the expression "Water, water, everywhere / Nor any drop to drink" has lingered in popular culture for over two hundred years attests to the power of its message.

Elastic Boundaries of Modernity

Just as water holds potential as a metaphoric device for understanding humanity, it also contains symbolic possibilities for grasping modernity. Modernity is caught between the fixed (its historical roots) and the fluid (the current global cultural order). The artists in *Water, Water Everywhere* . . . use new artistic vocabularies to challenge the stability of artistic modernity, offering what might be called alternative modernities.[6] They are socially engaged in the world and express this involvement through the flexible vehicle of art, a lens through which we can focus more clearly on the societies around us.[7]

Modernity is an ambitious utopian scheme based on philosophical ideals rooted in the Western Renaissance. Its values are radical: a preference for the chaos of the changing present over the fixities of the past; an openness to artistic forms outside of Western Europe; an interest in popular rather than "high" culture; a resistance to bourgeois capitalism which valued science and fact over mutable cultural meaning; and a mistrust of the notion of "rational" material and social progress.[8] Modernity flowed outward from its birthplace in France during its youthful years in the late nineteenth and early twentieth centuries. It was elastic and flexible, sustaining its formal vigor by absorbing the traditions and practices of other cultures.

As political modernity began to impose its own imperatives onto the governance structures of societies throughout the world, however, artistic modernity began to narrow the definition of legitimate art. The idea of modernity began to exclude some of the very forms that had given the movement its initial vital impulse. Artists turned their backs on indigenous artistic traditions and local histories. Artistic modernity became a colonizing force that affected the arts of non-Western practitioners, reducing their production to weak imitations of Western models.

In the 1960s modernity was almost one hundred years old, and its tenets had become static and brittle. However, monumental social changes revitalized it, making it again vulnerable to indigenous traditions: Buddhism and other Eastern religions; Jungian psychology; mythological systems other than those of Greece and Rome; and post-independence analysis from former colonies of the effects of imperialism on local philosophical and political practices. Modernity stretched to accommodate these ideas. It is this "adaptive" modernity that sets the stage for understanding the content and form of the works in *Water, Water Everywhere* . . . . [9]

Adaptive modernity has a countenance as changeable as that of water, as variable as the artists under its rubric. The most notable of these individuals hold ideas and form in tension and express something unique about contemporary life. Stan Douglas, for example, is "interested in finding forms of representation that have some structural relationship to the subject,"[10] a pursuit at the heart of the enterprise of adaptive modernity.

The predominance of video and sculpture in this exhibition reflects a correspondence of medium and subject. Video, like water, is characterized by mobility and permutation. The sculpture in the show suggests the temporary solidity of water in the form of ice, prone to alteration in response to the shifting conditions around it. As we "read" the sculpture on view, our perceptions of it change. The lone painter in the exhibition is Carrie Yamaoka, whose iridescent, shimmering surfaces change as rapidly as waves at the seashore. Painting is, perhaps, the medium most threatened by adaptive modernities, yet Yamaoka demonstrates the medium's flexibility by using non-painting materials to flirt with painting's "reflection" of contemporary society. Roni Horn's photographs of the river Thames question photography's ability to represent the vitality of nature, which she expresses through inversions in the relationship between image and text.

Perhaps the most urgent question regarding the globalized art world represented in *Water, Water Everywhere . . .* is: how can works from such disparate places of origin be intelligible to a local audience? Without a centralized codification of meaning, adaptive modernity demands a more rigorous interpretation of ideas on the part of its audience, whether here or abroad. Scottsdale is as foreign to people in Bangkok as Bangkok is to Scottsdale; we are equally responsible for deciphering the art works that connect us.

Samuel Taylor Coleridge's poem was completed within a decade of the historical event on which STAN DOUGLAS's *Nu•tka•*, 1996, is based. In 1789, British and Spanish ships converging on the shores of Vancouver Island represented two imperial powers looking to claim the land for their empires. The rival captains struggled for dominance, ignoring the native population living there. (In fact, the colonizers named the people and the bay Nutka, assuming that the word the locals used repeatedly was their name. Nutka, in fact, means "go" or "turn around."[11])

Douglas stages his "Canadian gothic"[12] at the border between land and sea of Nutka Bay. The scenery is literally split in two, the alternating bands of the image scrolling toward each other slowly, occasionally joining for a moment of resolution. The ghostly voice-overs—reading from the journals of the two competing captains—chart the descent into the madness of civilization, caused by imperialism's impact on colonized and colonizer. Rather than presenting the conventional heroic narrative of conquest, the work suggests instead "violence, fear, and utter hopeless confusion."[13] *Nu•tka•* embodies this moment of imperial aggression, when conflicting forces each teeter on the brink of success or failure, by exaggerating the physical and psychological split of the actors.[14]

This seemingly simple work contains many of the contradictions found throughout the show. Reacting to Douglas's work, curator Simon Watson wrote that "an appreciation of 'nature' in art must either negotiate or suppress the social and industrial conflicts that animate the history [of a place]."[15] Douglas wants to dispel any lingering remnants of the myth of the new world as a blank slate for exploitation by the old. He puts his work on an endless loop to suggest the persistence of patterns of human behavior.

The historical schism represented in Douglas's work occurred during a specific and, relatively speaking, recent wave of imperialism. Yet humans have sought to conquer and influence one another since the beginning of time. LARA BALADI's *Mother of the World #2 [Oum El Dounia]*, 2005, presents a staged enactment of cultural hybridity, in which the caterpillar from *Alice in Wonderland* mingles with a mermaid from Greek mythology. Baladi's polyglot appropriations, which unmoor figures from their contexts, are legible to us as "collective representations emanating from primeval dreams and creative fantasies."[16] Although Egypt's most familiar images—pyramids, hieroglyphs, Queen Nefertiri and Tutankhamum—date to well before waves of conquest by the Greeks, Romans, Arabs, French and English, they persist as archetypes across the globe.

Baladi has mounted billboard-sized works in urban spaces, such as Cairo's Tahrir Square (a major traffic hub and site of intermittent public protests), to acknowledge the public nature of her cultural mixes. Egyptian billboards are hand-painted, which lends them a quirky, personal quality. Their scale suggests the models of the Greek and Roman sculptural friezes that disseminated cultural traditions and European frescoes painted on the walls of medieval churches that educated illiterate citizens.

Baladi has created a new version of *Mother of the World #2* for the current exhibition, installing it within the galleries of the Scottsdale Museum of Contemporary Art. We gaze at a world above and beyond our own, looking at her characters, many of whom appear in multiple "scenes" across the screen. Baladi does not literally depict water; she evokes ancient trade routes in the image of rich, rippling sand and modern air travel in a deep blue sky. Travel here is an emotional, spiritual quest for love, safety and consciousness. Baladi's transposed sand and water are culturally specific elements that secure her floating figures. The elegant, humanist frieze describes a utopian world that promises hope of transformation and refuge. The artist's influences come from many different quarters, independent of the "directionality of change" in the world.[17]

Adaptive modernity allows for the integration of modern (read: Western) artistic practice with local traditions, as manifested in Baladi's playful work. Ultimately, she turns from the specifics of history to create a mellifluous blend of traditions. This dialectic—of modern and traditional, of open and closed borders—links many of the artists in the show. Baladi's metaphoric borrowings represent the most positive outcomes of globalization.

DOROTHY CROSS uses common materials and surreal juxtapositions to comment on politics, gender and sexuality in Irish culture. Her dreamlike video *Jellyfish Lake*, 2002, is an homage to amateur marine biologist Maude Delap, who lived in the late 19th century on Valentia Island (off the coast of Ireland). Delap bred and studied venomous jellyfish.[18] Although she sent the results of her study to the Natural History Museum of Ireland in Dublin, her scientific contribution was never acknowledged on account of her gender.

In *Jellyfish Lake*, we see a woman (Cross herself) floating in water, surrounded by thousands of translucent jellyfish. Her hair floats in an aureole around her head, suggesting Medusa. (The Latin name for jellyfish is *medusae*; literary references like this within scientific nomenclature reinforced gender-based stereotypes in the late 19th century.)[19] We watch, horrified and fascinated, as the creatures encircle the figure. Jellyfish Lake, located on Palau in the South Pacific, has long been separated from the ocean by land upheavals. The jellyfish there have no natural predators and hence have lost their sting. The woman and jellyfish float together in harmony, alluding by way of contrast to the harmful effects of the "objective" scientific practice of the past two centuries.

Despite the myth of the matriarchy in Ireland,[20] the Irish do not participate in Western Europe's "love affair" with the female form.[21] The repression of the body can be a repression of the mind.[22] Interestingly, Cross's brother, zoologist Tom Cross, was her collaborator on this work, a partnership that symbolically overcomes the inequity between the sexes that colored Delap's study of jellyfish.

Cross refers to another set of historical events in the video *Teapot*, 1997. On a small monitor, we see a teacup inside of which is a long rowboat that eventually capsizes in a stormy sea, losing its crew. The imagery, in combination with the title, sparks associations with the phrase "tempest in a teapot" and may thereby evoke William Shakespeare's *The Tempest* of 1611. The Shakespearean play is purportedly based on the true story of a British ship wrecked in Bermuda in 1609 on its way to colonize Virginia. The drama explores political greed and upheaval fraternal betrayal, exile, magic, ancient political relationships, filial devotion and the folly of humanity. The character Gonzalo expresses his frustration at being caught in a rigid social hierarchy and dreams of an island community with no servants, money, aristocracy or labor (where he would, incidentally, crown himself king).

Cross's coded choice of *The Tempest* as a subject involves the history of Ireland. The early 17th century saw the British enter the colonial race (already lagging behind the Portuguese and French) at the same time that the Irish were struggling for social and religious freedom from Britain. Imperialism has never been motivated by racist impulses alone—the Egyptians conquered the Nubians and the Japanese dominated the Chinese and Koreans. Gonzalo's wish to start a new republic on a deserted island may have represented a cherished dream to the Irish during the age of "discovery." Cross appropriates this well-known literary classic and compresses it into a teacup, a foremost emblem of the British. She literally pushes the British Empire back onto its own tiny island.

JUN NGUYEN-HATSUSHIBA calls on the ancient tradition of Vietnamese water puppetry to meditate on contemporary Vietnam, caught in the riptide of globalization. The water-puppet pageants of the Red River Delta were staged as an homage to the life-giving force of water which sustained Vietnamese civilization, and as an invocation to the otherworldly spirits of the land. Stages were built on water, with the puppeteers concealing their hands beneath the surface. They used special effects—such as artificially generated waves—to indicate the passage of time, water's animistic moods and the sweep of historical events.[23] Traditional water-puppet pageants told the myths of ancient Vietnam; Nguyen-Hatsushiba focuses on the myths of contemporary life,[24] using water to suggest suspension and unification.

In *Memorial Project Nha Trang, Vietnam Toward the Complex – For the Courageous, the Curious and the Cowards*, 2001, the first of his underwater works, Nguyen-Hatsushiba choreographs cyclo drivers pushing and pulling their vehicles across the sandy ocean floor. The cyclo, a three-wheeled bicycle cart for pulling people and goods, has been the predominant, low-cost mode of transportation in Vietnam for decades. The drivers in the video do not use any artificial means of oxygen supply; they must propel themselves to surface of the shallow water to gulp air, mirroring the cyclo drivers' struggle to survive in an environment now dominated by cars.

In an effort to modernize the country, the government banned cyclos in 2001, replacing the cost-effective and quiet mode of transportation with an expensive and polluting alternative. The cyclos represent a style of life and serve as a cog in the economic and social engine of the country, and the government was pressured into lifting the ban in 2003.

In *Memorial Project Nha Trang, Vietnam Toward the Complex – For the Courageous, the Curious and the Cowards*, the artist conveys the challenges of the present, but also memorializes the forgotten Vietnamese who died at sea while trying to escape the war.[25] Like Chris Burden and Maya Lin, who have also commemorated that controversial war with anti-monumental works, Nguyen-Hatsushiba honors the anonymous lives of those who struggled vainly for survival.

All of Nguyen-Hatsushiba's water-based works have a dreamlike quality. The murky green of water, the slow-motion movements and the jittery relationship between people and objects evoke the unstable relationship between lived experiences and recorded history. According to Jung, dreams are compensatory, transmitting "unconscious reactions or spontaneous impulses" to consciousness.[26] Nguyen-Hatsushiba's dreams bypass the realpolitik of Vietnam to connect people to their buried history. He asserts artistic self-definition in the face of Western cultural imperialism by combining the ancient and the new.

Water has always played a significant role in JANAINA TSCHÄPE's work. In a series of photographs from the early 1990s, the artist encased her feet, hands, legs and even her head in water-filled balloons. In later videos, she created bulbous costumes for female characters who languish at the boundary of water and land, seeming to dream of a past aquatic life.

Tschäpe's work *Blood, Sea*, 2004, is named after a short chapter in Italo Calvino's book *t zero*.[27] In Calvino's work, the narrator describes the moment when he is conscious of being part of primordial matter. Not yet evolved into a single-cell organism with a permeable boundary, the hero describes how a "sense" of differentiation was enough to make him wildly happy. This moment of consciousness was the beginning of the "I." By the end of the story, the narrator is a fully articulated and independent being, who describes this transition from non-being to being to children who would never experience the sense of awakened ego. Calvino's evolutionary scale starts with undifferentiated mass, moving to organisms in which air is encased in internal cavities and water becomes blood.

In *Blood, Sea*, Tschäpe immerses her characters in water,[28] dressed in elaborate costumes the artist designed herself: one is elegant in white, like the Nike of Samothrace; another, a black spider, cloaks herself in a long, tangled web; a third is covered by a transparent skin, stuffed with multicolored balloon "organs" that give her an alien form. When the figures are filmed from below, against the round rim of the pool, they seem to fly. When filmed from above, they float in rocky coral lairs. The pool has many moods: it is luminous under the light of the sky above, which lends an artificial magic to many scenes; it is ominous when light is absent. Columns of bubbles rise to the surface from the women breathing through air tubes, like tiny messages sent to the outside world. In Calvino's *Blood, Sea*, the author suggests that we are "swum by our environment"; Tschäpe's characters embody this notion.

In *Blood, Sea*, Tschäpe twists together genres as diverse as landscape photography, science fiction and televised nature shows—all notably different in social, political and class associations. The artist mixes cultural myths, expressing the Buddhist belief that "the work of nature and culture are interdependent."[29] Tschäpe refers not only to myths of origin, but also to the hybrid Brazilian religion that mixes European

Catholicism and traditional African practices. Tschäpe proposes that reunification through water might propel a reunification of culture.

Every society has specific traditions and symbols that are difficult to read from the outside. Writing about a popular television show in China, Xiaomei Chen states that official and anti-official Occidentalism use "superficially similar sign systems that can be manipulated for very different ideological ends."[30] The notion that ideas or ideological concepts are never either intrinsically oppressive or liberating allows artists like SONG DONG to insert culturally specific criticisms into globally legible works.[31] Song Dong tries to bridge the schism between collective and individual memory, between the disappearance of old China and the appearance of the new city, and between the self and the state.[32] His elegant, fluid works are not agitprop. He combines a Buddhist understanding of the fleeting nature of human life, a generous grasp of the impulses behind human activity and a wry appreciation of the value of human labor (art included).

Song has long consulted water as a vehicle for his spiritual ruminations. His art functions as both a social demonstration and a gesture of healing. Works such as *Breathing*, 1996, function as social interventions designed to create a small fissure in the enormous edifice of Chinese society. In *Breathing*, Song lay in a deserted Tiananmen Square, and then by the Back Sea (another Beijing landmark), just after midnight on New Year's Day. He melted the thin sheets of ice on the ground with his warm breath. The small change his body made on the two sites—one the symbol of state strength, the other an important social symbol—commemorated the demonstrators of the June 4, 1989 movement for a more open government.

Song produced the video installation *Floating: Scottsdale* for *Water, Water Everywhere*. . . . He filmed the city on foot and by car, then layered this footage with shots of himself as he traced numbers in water onto which the cityscape was reflected. In *Floating: Scottsdale*, the city shimmers like a mirage that is interrupted by the touch of a hand. As a visitor, Song cannot really "know" Scottsdale; the meaning of the city shifts and sways. Millions know the southwest only through the ephemeral images brought to them through television and film, yet these images cannot present what is real. He points out that it is impossible for us to grasp all dimensions of our environments—whether they be Scottsdale or Beijing—as they undergo rapid development. The two cities could not be more dissimilar, yet Song finds commonality through his use of light and water.

Finnish artist LAURA HORELLI explores the dynamics of human, social and natural landscapes in the globalized world.[33] She has studied the effects of mobile-phone use on different generations of Finns and the impact of women leaders from the Third World on the international political stage. For Horelli, such public issues have private ramifications.

Horelli continues tracing social constructs in *Helsinki Shipyard / Port San Juan*, 2003, in which she juxtaposes interviews with the makers of luxury cruise liners, most of whom are Finnish, with those of the multinational employees who work in the ships' bowels. The artist was interested in the way "two diverse groups of workers, those within the nation-state based heavy industry and those in the global, multi-ethnic service industry, are linked to the same objects of the cruise ship."[34] Issues of class, workers' rights and the commodification of water inform the work.

The steel workers, engineers, interior designers and factory managers in Finland who create the ships are "alienated" from their products: there is no tradition of luxury cruises in Europe, and Nordic design is typically "plain and practical. . . . Many of the builders referred to the interiors as being too American." There is a long history of shipbuilding in Finland—it has been an important economic factor since the 1700s—but the post–World-War-II industry was controlled by the Soviet Union, who awarded shipbuilding contracts to the Finns as war reparations. Finnish shipyards today specialize in high-tech construction, but their production has dwindled from 40% of the world's ships to 10%, supplanted by Asian manufacturers. Horelli's subjects are concerned about the economic viability of their profession within the shifting global economy.

The crews that work these huge cruise vessels are multinational, although English is the *lingua franca* on board. In the interviews, they discuss the practicalities of moving tourists around—tending to massive volumes of luggage and the entertainment of repeat passengers no longer enthralled with exotic ports of call—and the impact this work has on their lives. How do they endure being on board and on call twenty-four hours a day? What is the ultimate reward of such poorly paid employment? The crew cite travel and getting to know people from other parts of the world as the most gratifying parts of their jobs. Cruise ships are largely registered in "flag-of-convenience" (FOC) countries that are known for the "laxness of their tax, labor, and regulatory law."[35] Companies circumvent systems that protect workers on land; at sea, the crew is virtually imprisoned on the luxurious boats for months at a time, without breaks.

Sociologist Robert E. Wood has written about cruise tourism as the future face of globalization. The industry represents "an independence of capital from its space-bound ties to employees, communities, places, and nations."[36] Water travel, once the dominion of fishermen, explorers, military personnel and immigrants, now represents conspicuous consumption. Low wages make the cost of passage widely affordable. Horelli compares the attitudes of the two groups of employees toward their industry and the quality of life it provides for them, and highlights the reality of water-based global cultural tourism.

ANGE LECCIA creates sculptural situations and filmic interventions. His sculptural "arrangements" are, typically, objects paired and facing each other. These found items include Super-8 projectors, electronic sound equipment and other media-related material.[37] Additional objects—jet fighters and dump trucks—are associated with the military-industrial complex. Leccia's subtle political commentary forms the intellectual undertow of his works. His filmic installations have nothing of his sculpture's materiality; he looks at nature's ephemeral effects—thunderstorms, clouds, dusk, water and light. Yet the artist invites political readings of his moody land- and seascapes by inserting into them historical and political situations, such as a decisive battle or the resistance mounted against a conquering nation.

For *The Sea [La Mer]*, 2001, Leccia filmed a beach from above. He projects the image in a vertical format against a wall. The crests of the waves, endlessly reconfiguring themselves, form a dancing line of foam. Like Sisyphus, they never reach the top of the screen. Formally, *The Sea* recalls the craggy abstract landscapes of Clyfford Still, but its blue palette makes it sensuous where Still's canvases are bleak.

Leccia was born and raised on Corsica, a small island nation subjected to numerous invaders over the centuries and currently seeking freedom from France. Leccia suggests that islands can be either safe havens or prisons. He literalizes this dichotomy by projecting a wall of water onto a vertical surface. The constant motion of the waves is comforting; it blocks out the harsh realities of daily life. As with many of his other installations, Leccia uses light to represent the ephemerality of meaning and social constructs.

Throughout her far-ranging oeuvre—which includes sculpture, photography, artist's books and multimedia installations—RONI HORN treats the living (people, nature) and the inert (taxidermied animals) with the same detached curiosity. She often works in series, which provide viewers with multiple images to compare and contrast. By presenting many versions of the same scene or subject, Horn reinforces the notion that time, space and random thoughts divert us from the subject at hand. In fact, in spite of the cumulative information the artist presents, it seems the closer you get to her subject, the farther it recedes.[38] Horn's perpetual subject is the moving target of identity.

Water has become important to Horn: she states that it represents a "symbol for the ambiguity of things that are both themselves and something more."[39] In the series of fifteen offset lithographs that constitute *Still Water (The River Thames, For Example)*, 1999, Horn projects onto the river the broadest possible range of human emotions. We see the Thames in its various miens, under different weather conditions. It is gloomy, murky, viscous and polluted; cheery, fast and clean; spiritual, calming and ageless. The repeated images roll slowly by like a film.

The surface of each work is dotted with tiny white numbers. These act as footnotes to the statements and ruminations on language, images and self set below the prints, which the artist both wrote herself and culled from published sources. The writing is alternately philosophical, humorous and rhetorical. The language mimics the variable countenance of the river itself. In *Still Water (The River Thames, For Example)*, Image E, Horn writes: "12. Are you thinking Claude Monet, too?"; "19. When you go into the river you discover a new entrance—and in yourself you uncover an exit, an unseen exit, your exit. (You brought it with you.)"; and "27. Police pieced together a story from a trail of eyewitness accounts about a man going straight from afternoon prayer at the mosque at Parsons Green to the river. He wrote a suicide note and slipped it into his shirt pocket (never found). He left his shoes and socks neatly arranged on the bank." Each entry plays with narrative constructs that evoke different aspects of the world.

By pairing image and text in a deadpan way, Horn participates in a long artistic tradition that questions the "truthfulness" of photography. Her series points to the difficulty of using words (one system of abstraction) to describe a photograph (another system altogether). Additionally, the artist comments on the impossibility of capturing the "life" of anything in a photograph. Any picture of nature renders the rich life of the subject a *nature morte*—dead nature.

CARRIE YAMAOKA also unpacks the structures built up around a specific art form so she can reconfigure them. Yamaoka rejects painting's historical function as a "window on the world." She uses non-painting materials to break with the tradition; her works are more appropriately described as "constructed." The artist is dedicated to recasting the dialogue around a reified art form that has been so rooted firmly in the Western lexicon of high art.

Yamaoka uses beauty as a hook to engage the viewer in her works.[40] She begins each piece by building a wooden frame into which she pours a layer of tinted resin. (How does one contain a liquid? Ask the Army Corp of Engineers.) On top of this she lays a sheet of mylar—sometimes flattened, occasionally with folds and bubbles. She completes the work with another pour of tinted resin. She breaks the barrier between sculpture and painting; the works are flexible, hanging from the wall with Velcro.

The distinction between representation and abstraction is put to rest in these works; they are both and neither. *Kool Pop #18*, 2004, provokes subtle associations: its wrinkled milky-green surface resembles the bottom of a kid's inflatable swimming pool, the optical effects of silt in a mountain lake, the quality of semiprecious stones or the mournful eyes of a blind dog. In *68 by 12 (blue.green)*, 2005, Yamaoka lustily embraces water: the seductive, rich blue surface proclaims its beauty. The work begins sedately enough on the wall, then drapes down to rest on the floor. It is humorous: think of a cartoon character's jaw dropping open, the tongue unfurling like a New Year's Eve noisemaker. *68 by 12 (blue.green)* is not a sculptural installation; the work is still firmly attached to the notion of painting on the wall.

The surfaces of her works are invisible to Yamaoka as she's making them (chance plays a role in determining the look of the piece). Of course, skill and experimentation allow the artist to "direct" the result to some degree. Bubbles in the resin, folds in the mylar, a crease in the bottom layer of plastic that holds the resin and differences in the density of tint and scale contribute to the range of effects. Chance was used by the Surrealists in the early 20th century (under the influence of psychoanalysis and the interpretation of dreams) as a way to resist the noose of rational Western scientific thought. Using systems that are seemingly "irrational" (to Western eyes) loosens modernity's grip, allowing artists to avoid the strict "master" narrative of artistic genius.

The illusive space Yamaoka creates distorts us like a rippling pond or a fun-house mirror. Yet her works are highly social; they reflect the space and viewers around them and change in response to different light conditions. Yamaoka's paintings engender multiple readings over time. (Who hasn't sat staring at waves crashing on the beach, hoping to fix one particular image among the infinite moments?) The painting's identity remains in flux, one of the primary subjects of this exhibition.

Throughout his career, ROBERT GOBER has created mute, melancholic, figurative sculptures that reflect Western society's schizophrenic attitudes toward desire and sin. Raised in a Catholic home, Gober gives evidence of his religious upbringing in many of his works. Water's symbolic power to absolve plays a central role in his oeuvre. Gober purifies a certain type of sin (that of homosexuality) through his own form of artistic confession. Overall, he challenges the "naturalness of social construction" by cross-fertilizing many symbolic systems—artistic, social and cultural.[41]

Despite the mysterious quality of Gober's works, he himself is very deliberate about his intentions. He conjoins surrealism and minimalism in a way that violates the received wisdom of both. Gober is interested in things that "flow beneath the everyday," and his objects are all props from the "American Gothic" sitcom we call contemporary society.[42] He makes all of his objects by hand. In doing so, he rejects the mass-production and consumption predilections of the culture. He returns to the Protestant work ethic of efficacy, but from a feminine—not a rugged male—perspective. Gober's linguistic and visual punning, and his interest in gender confusion, give an American twist to Marcel Duchamp's witty inventions.

Since the early 1980s Gober has created sinks without water or plumbing, culverts that connect to nothing, and drains and storm grates that do not vent. His mountain cascades and filled bathtubs endlessly recycle water. The "X" of Gober's drain can be read as a prohibition against sex, and the sewer refers to illicit behavior. His drains are stigmata-like holes through which the body politic can be drained of its disease.

Untitled, 2004, is a bronze-cast piece of driftwood that may once have belonged to a dock stairway, based on the evidence of traces of cross-bracing. This work is ghostly, with abstract and figurative associations. The hard, slick surface of the plank is marred by small barnacles (like the lesions that mark some people with AIDS). It leans alone against the wall, like a despondent streetwalker or hospital patient awaiting treatment.

Gober's oftentimes barren objects are his response, as a gay man, to the societal censure of nontraditional lifestyles. Jung said the diseasing of the social body is a "disease of attitude."[43] The AIDS crisis is treated as a punishment from God when, in fact, it came into existence as a result of man's manipulation of nature. Jung's "disease of attitude" refers to modern society's amnesia in the face of ancient social and natural values, which included acceptance of others. Gober too describes a world diseased by attitude. His frequent use of and reference to water symbolizes salvation. Gober refers to our common origins and archetypes while trying to build a new, improved mythology.

TONY FEHER's interests range from macro-processes of nature (such as evaporation) to the mega-complexities of contemporary society (such as the craze for bottled water). His elegant minimalist sculptures display common materials in repetitive, serial ways. A simple line of objects achieve the kind of weighty volume created by the string drawings of Fred Sandback. Artists have used found objects since the beginning of the 20th century to articulate a variety of intentions. Feher wants each object to become part of our poetic landscape, one that evades the straight line of narrative meaning.[44]

Feher was first known for using one of the most unobtrusive, though hardly neutral, items in our landscape: the plastic bottle. He manipulates space with other materials as well—fancy colored glass bottles, rusty tin cans, packing foam, discarded radio antennas and plastic milk crates—compressing them, putting them on the ground or suspending them against the sky. Each piece suggests different social and political ideas. A plastic container hanging by a string from its crooked neck recalls the horrific lynchings in the United States in the early 20th century. Feher also considers how we smother the earth with garbage and extract its resources in order to, say, deliver cheap soda.

For the SMoCA show, Feher created a series of works specifically for this exhibition, using materials gleaned during his second visit to Scottsdale and others he has collected over the past few years. Working against all the traditional methods of making sculpture, Feher creates multiple moments of small pleasure and discovery. An electrical plug covered with blue tape recalls spring ponds which fill, then slowly evaporate and muddy as the freshness of spring evolves into the heavy heat of summer. Irregular tears of plastic resemble the translucent rains of spring that waver and shift with the wind.

Through the spatial organization of the piece, which forces us to look up and to bow down, the artist cleverly suggests a spiritual or ritualistic dimension in the experience of art viewing. Aware of the thin line between spirituality and superstition, Feher does not emphasize this aspect of the work. He is more concerned with representing water itself, in a nonliteral way. The material properties of plastic and water are such that they share a similarly tenuous distinction between inside and out, solid and liquid, fixed and fluid.

Early modernists like Pablo Picasso used non-Western visual vocabularies (whether antique Iberian sculpture or Japanese woodblock prints) to break Western art's attachment to representation. For over a decade, JACCI DEN HARTOG, too, has worked with non-Western vocabularies as a way to "sculpt the unsculptable," to capture that which is hidden rather than to render abstractly that which is real.[45] In particular, she refers to Eastern gardens, and the landscape paintings and *ukiyo-e* prints that depict them. Den Hartog sculpts, casts and then paints her resin-based landscape sculptures. Their surprising forms depart in formal qualities from much traditional sculpture.

In her seascape sculptures, which she began in the late 1990s, Den Hartog renders visible the features that shape the surface contours of water: air currents, foam caps, surges and rocks on the ocean floor that cause eddies and ripples. The mood ranges from angry or menacing to placid and sunny. Her rivers flow down from the mountains to the ocean—a slight tinge of color suggests the vanishing point of perspectival space. Den Hartog's works resemble the reverse-contoured oceanscapes found at small aquariums. The sculptures are oddly serene, holding the movement of life in stasis. The suspended energy makes the works excessive, almost baroque, despite the minimalist presentation. Chinese gardens are designed to make a small space seem big; we do not see the whole landscape when we are in it.[46] Den Hartog, by contrast, scales her works so that you sense the vastness of the ocean and feel the distance of the endlessly receding horizon.

For Den Hartog, the ocean represents our fear of unknown forces, as its scale and power dwarf human civilization. Each of the waist-high works triggers for the viewer a kinesthetic memory of standing in a pond, soaked to the skin. Den Hartog, who has lived a few miles from the California beach for decades, pays homage to the romantic ideal of the ocean she rarely visits.

RIVANE NEUENSCHWANDER uses simple found materials, tiny living creatures and processes of nature to suggest the melancholy of life. She relates art to nature's "perpetual transformations."[47] Her deliberate experiments—seemingly random—demonstrate the search for an alternative order of meaning in the world, one that reconciles nature and culture.

Neuenschwander has often used the behaviors of unwitting creatures (snails, ants, fish) to constitute the process for her work. In *Love Lettering*, 2002, tiny goldfish swim back and forth across the blue expanse of a fish tank. With her brother, a neuroscientist, Neuenschwander attached small pieces of paper inscribed with words to the fish's fins. The concrete poetry that results, randomly generated by the swimming creatures, hints at love and longing. It is accompanied by melodic sounds that reinforce the trancelike quality of the movements.

Travel, displacement and diaspora are at the heart of much of Neuenschwander's work. The melancholy comes from the overwhelming sense of loss—of family history, of loved ones, of place—within the shifting global sphere. As an artist, Neuenschwander has the privilege to be nomadic; other people around the world have to move simply to survive.[48] With each of our arrivals and departures, our sense of place and self slips a little farther beyond our grasp. Neuenschwander gently probes the negative side of modern travel and diaspora.

In *Belong, Not Belong*, 2000, a grid of nine photographs shows shiny black beetles playing with transparent bubbles. The bugs recall old-fashioned muscle men in gymnasiums, ancient knights fighting the devil in one of his guises or a biology class experiment. In each scenario the bugs are heroic, but doomed.

SABRINA MEZZAQUI works with a wide range of materials to explore the vocabularies of social intercourse and domestic ornamentation, as well as the delicacy of private life. Each investigation requires new materials and skills. Her minimalist objects are fraught with evocative content. She merges personal memories and history—a history of "imaginative projection."[49] Mezzaqui looks at the world as measured by individual experience, not by the grand sweep of world events.

In *A Thousand and One Nights—Radio Tunisia [Le mille e una notte—Radio Tunisi]*, 1999, a sparkling sea fills a small screen. Viewers might recall a glorious summer day at the beach or their first childhood visit to the shore: the combination of sunlight and water provokes almost universally a joyous response to their life-giving properties. In the piece, an Arabic pop tune "JSK (Jeunesse Sportive de Kabylie) [Sports Youth of Kabylie]" by Abdelli (an Algerian Berber) accompanies the dancing sea. The soccer team JSK was formed in 1946 in Tizi-Ouzou. Like other Muslim soccer clubs in Algeria, it suspended play during the Algerian war of independence (1954–1962).[50] In the song, Abdelli uses Algeria's struggle for independence as a mirror for his own ethnic group's demand for recognition.

The Berbers are a North African tribal society with origins dating to 2400 B.C.E., whose rights have been limited by the ethnic Arab majority. Dan Nghiem Van has written: "Ethnic-group-origin tales have reason to stress a single common origin for all groups in a country that has suffered continually from foreign invasions."[51] Despite the role that the Berbers played in overturning French rule in Algeria, they face a second wave of discrimination by fellow countrymen.

The soundtrack of *A Thousand and One Nights—Radio Tunisia* creates an additional dimension for understanding. Like the sounds of water gently lapping at a pond's shore, the crash of the ocean's waves, heavy raindrops pelting a roof, or dishwater flowing into the drain, Abdelli's infectious song infiltrates our subconscious. The story framing *A Thousand and One Nights* is that of Scheherazade, a vizier's daughter who volunteers to marry King Shahryar despite the fact that, in response to the infidelity of his first spouse, he kills his wives after one night. Scheherazade entertains him with fabulous tales, staying her execution each night by leaving him with a cliffhanger. She proves her loyalty and love, bearing the king three children during the length of her tale and saving her life and those of countless other women. Mezzaqui draws a parallel between the plight and survival strategies of the Berbers and those of Scheherazade through the bright image of water and the hopeful sounds of music.

CONCLUSION

The philosopher Immanuel Kant proposed that the cosmopolitan law of "universal hospitality" was rooted in the "finitude of the earth."[52] As the world shrinks through travel and communication, it becomes urgent that we understand "finitude." The degradation and imbalance we have created in our natural environment, added to the demands of an expanding population, require new solutions to common problems, whether political, social or cultural.

There are innumerable idioms in the English language alone that allude to water: "sea of humanity," "cry me a river," "capital flow," "floodgate of emotions," "like oil and water," and so on. Water metaphors are everywhere in culture. Jung said that we have lost the power to perceive symbols because we have lost our connection to the earth. We are born with psyches loaded with instincts or impulses that are generally so buried and remote as to be unknowable until dreams reveal their meaning.[53] Art can similarly unlock subconscious meanings, and give depth to the recurrent symbols of our time.

Notes

Roni Horn in *Focus: Roni Horn*, exh. brochure (Chicago: Art Institute of Chicago, 2004), n.p.

World Spirituality, vol. 8, *Buddhist Spirituality: Indian, Southeast Asian, Tibetan, Early Chinese*, ed. Takeuchi Yoshinori (New York: Crossroad Publishing, 1993).

West Marrin, *Universal Water: The Ancient Wisdom and Scientific Theory of Water* (Makawao, Hawaii: Inner Ocean, 2002), 9–24.

Dang Nghiem Van, "The Flood Myth and the Origin of Ethnic Groups in Southeast Asia," *Journal of American Folklore* 106 (1993), 318.

[5] Samuel Taylor Coleridge (1772–1834) was an English Romantic poet, critic and philosopher.

[6] Dilip Parameshwar Gaonkar, "On Alternative Modernities," in Gaonkar, ed., *Alternative Modernities* (Durham, North Carolina: Duke University Press, 2001), 12.

[7] Ibid., 1–23.

[8] Ibid.

[9] Samir Khalaf, *Cultural Resistance: Global Encounters in the Middle East* (London: Saqi Books, 2001), 56, citing John Lewis, "The Social Limits of Politically Induced Change," in Chandler Morse et al., eds., *Modernization by Design* (Ithaca: Cornell University Press, 1969).

[10] Diana Thater, "Diana Thater in Conversation with Stan Douglas," in Scott Watson, with Diana Thater and Carol J. Clover, *Stan Douglas* (London: Phaidon Press, 1998), 12.

[11] Quoted in Watson, Thater and Clover, *Stan Douglas*, 132.

[12] Douglas describes Gothic romance as "typically characterized by a return of the repressed: some past transgression haunts, then destroys the culpable person, family or social order. It is no surprise that these narratives flourished during the era of high imperialism—when remote and exotic areas of the world were being drawn into the European orbit. . . . What would contact and mingling with radically foreign cultures bring?" Ibid.

[13] Murray Whyte, "A Disorienting Vision of Unchecked Progress," *National Post*, Oct. 1, 1999.

[14] Thater, "Conversation," 29.

[15] Simon Watson, "Against the Habitual," in Watson, Thater and Clover, *Stan Douglas*, 66.

[16] Carl G. Jung et al, *Man and His Symbols* (Garden City, New York: DoubleDay, 1964), 55.

[17] Khalaf, *Cultural Resistance*, 54.

[18] Isabel Nolan, "Crossing the Great Divide," *Irish Arts Review* 19, no. 1. (Summer 2002), 54–57.

[19] James Hall, *Dictionary of Subjects and Symbols in Art* (New York: Icon Editions, Harper & Row Publishers, 1974; rev. ed., 1979), 206.

[20] See Cheryl Herr, "The Erotics of Irishness," in Kwame Anthony Appiah and Henry Louis Gates, Jr., eds., *Identities* (Chicago: University of Chicago Press, 1995), 293–94, citing Rosita Sweetman's *On Our Backs: Sexual Attitudes in a Changing Ireland* (London: Pan Books, 1979).

[21] Ibid, 285.

[22] Ibid, 276.

[23] Gloria Contreras, "Teaching about Vietnamese Culture:

Water is relevant not only to desert cities like Scottsdale, but critical to survival everywhere on earth. Artists are uniquely able to reconcile the universal (such as the need for water) and the specific (local traditions and rituals based on water). The artists in *Water, Water Everywhere . . .* correlate content and form to mediate the conflicting, chaotic ideas of the present. They wrestle with quixotic notions such as historical "truth" and the collective unconscious so that we can see the world through a different lens. We are left with a more fluid, spiritual and expansive understanding of human behavior than our fact-driven society customarily encourages. These adaptive modernities allow for a new grasp of our connected world.

Water Puppetry as the Soul of the Rice Fields," *Social Studies* 86 (Jan./Feb. 1995), 25–28.

[24] Ibid.

[25] Jun Nguyen-Hatsushiba, e-mail message to author, Mar. 18, 2005, copy in author's files.

[26] Jung, *Man and His Symbols*, 67.

[27] Italo Calvino, *t zero* (New York: Harcourt, Brace and World, 1969).

[28] *Blood, Sea* was filmed at a mermaid theme park in Weeki Wachee Springs, Florida.

[29] Donald K. Swearer, "Principles and Poetry, Places and Stories: The Resources of Buddhist Ecology" (1998), *Daedalus* 30 (Fall 2001), 227.

[30] Xiaomei Chen, "Occidentalism as Counterdiscourse: 'He Shang' in Post-Mao China," in Appiah and Gates, *Identities*, 70.

[31] Ibid.

[32] Wu Hung, "Between Past and Future: A Brief History of Contemporary Chinese Photography," in *Between Past and Future: New Photo and Video from China*, exh. cat. (Chicago, New York and Göttingen, Germany: David and Alfred Smart Museum of Art, International Center of Photography and Steidl Publishers, 2004), 26.

[33] Lucia Cerizza, "Interview with Laura Horelli and Deborah Ligoria," *Neue Review* 7 (Sept. 2004), 8–9.

[34] Laura Horelli, e-mail message to author, Mar. 6, 2005, copy in author's files. Subsequent remarks and quotations regarding the work are from this source unless otherwise noted.

[35] Robert E. Wood, "Globalization at Sea: Cruise Ships and the Deterritorialization of Capital, Labor, and Place" (MS, lecture, Eastern Sociological Society meeting, Baltimore, March 2000), 3, http://crab.rutgers.edu/~wood/cruise.doc.

[36] Ibid, 2.

[37] Eric Troncy, "Réalité contre réalité," *Numéro*, no. 55 (Aug. 2004), 200–05.

[38] Johanna Burton, "Review," *Time Out New York*, Nov. 15–22, 2001.

[39] Lyle Rexer, "Eye in the Labyrinth," *Art on Paper* 7, no.7 (May/June 2003), 54–55.

[40] Carrie Yamaoka, interview by the author, New York, Nov. 17, 2004.

[41] Maureen P. Sherlock, "Arcadian Elegy: The Art of Robert Gober," *Arts Magazine* 64 (Sept. 1989), 46.

[42] Richard Flood, "Interview: Richard Flood and Robert Gober," from *Robert Gober: Sculpture + Drawing*, exh. cat. (Minneapolis: Walker Art Center, 1999), 129.

[43] Jung, *Man and His Symbols*, 83.

[44] Adam Weinberg, "An Archeologist of His Own Life: Tony Feher in Conversation with Adam Weinberg," in *Tony Feher*, exh. cat. (Annandale-on-Hudson, New York: Bard College Center for Curatorial Studies, 2001), 61.

[45] Jacci Den Hartog, interview by the author, Los Angeles, Oct. 26, 2004.

[46] Ibid.

[47] Jens Hoffmann, "Rivane Neuenschwander: Ethereal Materi-

References

Portions of this essay were first published in *Mesh* #17,
<http://www.experimenta.org/mesh/mesh17/index.htm>,
Melbourne: Experimenta.org, 2004.

Art AsiaPacific, no. 37 (2003).

Philip Fisher, *The Vehement Passions* (Princeton: Princeton
University Press, 2002).

Craig Owens, *Beyond Recognition: Representation, Power, and
Culture* (Berkeley: University of California Press, 1992).

and aura work to mystify the source of their power. And while Ho unpacks or demystifies these processes of seduction, he doesn't in the end undermine them; or at least, one can leave *Utama* knowing that the desire for origins (for national history, for the originality of the work of art) is a phantasm, an impossibility. One also leaves with the pleasure of "presence," of being with the work of art.

Finally, there is another word, more closely associated with the notion of "aura" perhaps than "charisma," that I would like to mention—it is "wonder." Philip Fisher has written that the "passion of wonder has always been described by scientists and mathematicians as the heart of the experience of the search for new knowledge. . . . Wonder occurs at the horizon line of what is potentially knowable, but not yet known." If, as Fisher is suggesting, wonder is foundational to scientific inquiry, to the discovery of knowledge itself, then I want to add that wonder is also foundational to the process of critical inquiry. Too much contemporary writing about art (and not just about contemporary art but about art of all times) suffers from want of rigor and forcefulness of critique. There are no rules for writing short texts on art, but if I may say something as a guideline, if only to myself, it would be that what's essential to convey is a sense of being precariously on the horizon line of insight and judgement. The art criticism I want to write has, as its central object, the experience of wonder.

Tzu-Nyen Ho, *Utama-Every Name in History Is I*, 2003, poster, on exhibition at The Substation, Singapore, 2003. Photo: Amos Wong, digitally processed by Tzu-Nyen Ho.

3. The Impossible Origins of Water

Tzu-Nyen Ho's *Utama—Every Name in History Is I* was co-presented by The Substation arts center in 2003. The installation split the long gallery space into two sections: there was a screening room, where a twenty-minute DV film was shown that told the story of Sang Nila Utama, the mythical founder of Singapore. It was Utama who allegedly gave the island its name, "lion city" (from the Sanskrit words *singa* and *pura*). In the rest of the gallery, paintings were hung on the walls and lit from below with floodlights. The paintings looked "old," as if Ho had emulated the styles of 18th- and 19th-century European painting. The subjects of the portraits were historical figures, modeled by the actors in the film. There was, of course, Utama himself, but also Alexander the Great, Stamford Raffles and Vasco de Gama, among others. Their relationships to each other were (re)framed by the narrative of Ho's film; indeed, the paintings were film stills-cum-paintings, and the film, a painting-cum-moving picture.

The look of the paintings—their aura of European old masters—was achieved through digital technology. Ho appropriated images from canonical European artworks, printed them, and then painted over them, with the final effect that the pictures appear as if they were, thoroughly, entirely, painted. Although I don't think that Ho meant to simply fool his audiences—because, as I understand his intentions, the point is to generate ambiguity; to perfectly pass as the real thing is not as interesting. To experience *Utama* is to entertain doubt about the authenticity of Ho's paintings. The question is not whether they are forgeries of other known paintings—even though there is the issue of his borrowing from old masters—rather, the question is, what is their status as paintings? Which is perhaps the right question to ask, since the existence of his subject, Utama, is itself in question. Let me quote Ho at length, as he situates his work quite nicely:

> In official accounts of its history, Singapore was founded in 1819 by Sir Thomas Stamford Raffles, as part of the British colonial empire. However, little is known about the other, pre-colonial founder of Singapore, who is believed to have founded Singapore sometime between the 13th and 14th century. Commonly referred to as Sang Nila Utama, regarded as the "first" king of the Malays and said to be heir to a glorious lineage of great kings and immortals, he was said to have given Singapore its name after encountering a lion along its shores. . . . [This] event has often been questioned because lions are not a species indigenous to this area. For many historians, Utama's existence is itself a major issue of doubt—he was known under a variety of names and pseudonyms, and attributed with a multiplicity of identities and stories, many of which are contradictory in nature. . . . This film is an attempt to summon forth the specter of Utama—but he does not return alone. Instead he returns with an unruly host of characters, fictional, mystical and historical. Ultimately this is a film about the intertwining of myth and history, the impossibility of ontology, the instability of all beginnings.

It isn't hard to see how *Utama* might speak to the works in *Water, Water Everywhere* . . . . I'm thinking particularly of Stan Douglas's *Nu•tka•*, which also addresses themes of colonization and naming, and Lara Baladi's *Mother of the World #2*, which, as Knode notes, "presents a staged enactment of cultural hybridity." In myth, the Malay king Sang Nila Utama is cast as the authentic founder—as opposed to the colonial Raffles—of what would become a modern multicultural nation. It's important to realize that in the official discourses of Singapore, "multiculturalism" is effectively writ as a "multiracialism" that presumes a certain originary purity of the various Malay, Chinese and Indian source civilizations. But, again, what Ho's story presents to us is an Utama whose status is far from clear or pure.

Even though *Utama* is profoundly structured and informed by theory, what I like about it is that it never advertises its use theory. Most importantly, the film script is well-crafted, intelligent and very funny. *Utama* is a work that is self-conscious—but not self-indulgent—about the seductive powers of film and painting. One could say the former works through charisma, and the latter through aura. Aura entails the reverential, sometimes ecstatic, recognition of high cultural value, and charisma pertains to the attractive powers of personalities, or rather their images. Both charisma raises in her essay: "Perhaps the most urgent question regarding the globalized art world represented in *Water, Water Everywhere* . . . is: how can works from such disparate places of origin be intelligible to a local audience?" In talking about prepositions, I'm precisely concerned with the intelligibity of art writing across the distance of different social and cultural contexts. As Knode further states, "Without a centralized codification of meaning, adaptive modernity demands a more rigorous interpretation of ideas on the part of its audience, whether here or abroad. Scottsdale is as foreign to people in Bangkok as Bangkok is to Scottsdale; we are equally responsible for deciphering the art works that connect us."

How I propose to relate my own topic to the watery theme of this exhibition can be encapsulated by the phrases "these waters" and "universal water." Water has been a profound connector and transformer, a universal, so to speak, of human history. It has forced contact and conflict between different societies; where there is water, there is always some mediation, and, very importantly, some pressure. But we also refer to certain waters as being part of a place—thus, there are "these waters." Somehow, however, the claim never seems adequate: how can one put boundaries on open water? And still we do, although I think the point here is not that it's odd to territorialize the seas, but that all our markers of place are awkward.

Not so long ago, *Art AsiaPacific* published a special issue in which twenty-one curators and art writers each wrote about three artists of their choice. A number of these short texts started with the claim that so-and-so "is one of the most interesting artists from X." The problem isn't just that this is one of the worst ways to persuade a reader that the artist in question is actually interesting; what's worse is the inadvertent implication that these artists are notable primarily insofar as they represent their respective non-Western countries. The artists whom I've followed most closely over the years, regardless of where they're from, are never interested in speaking *for* their countries or for any category of identity. Invariably, their relationships to location are complicated; nonetheless, I don't recall any of them ever apologizing for the fact that they speak *from* specific situations. Craig Owens, citing Michel Foucault, once wrote about the "indignity of speaking for others"; it's a good reminder for art writers: to speak from, and of, but not for the people who make art, or for the places where they live and work.

But speaking *of* these particular places is not enough. There is also a universal imperative to speak *to* each other. The short text may have its limitations, but the more problematic default that prevails, not only in Singapore, but throughout the art world at large, is a well-meaning but flawed relativism. Relativism maintains that there are no non subjective perspectives, and opposes the ideal of an objective history. This is a misleading opposition. The practical and ethical challenge of writing from a given place isn't in trying to present the one true version of history, but in trying to speak truthfully from within a specific situation. Subjectivity is not an alibi for disengaging from this struggle for "truthfulness." The problem with relativism is that it does not provide the grounds on which to debate difference. In contrast, an ethics, which is suggested by the word "truthful," is predicated exactly on such an effort—these grounds may be as un-solid as water, as they are always provisional and situational, but for a specific moment in history, they are exemplary expressions of the commitment to speak *to* all others, not merely *from* where one speaks but *across* any difference.

There is another register involved in speaking *to*. Too much writing about contemporary art is reductive, telling the reader what the work is *about*. This closes off the experience of the work, when the main job of art writing should be to speak *to* a work of art, not *about* it. This isn't to say that one should be on the side of experience against theory. The contextual and theoretical framing that often takes up a large part of short essays is necessary and I would be loathe to dispense with it. Once a framework is laid out, however, often there isn't much space left over in a short essay, and all one can do is describe the work, without enough analysis. But what one can try to do, especially in brief texts, is to elect certain artworks as exemplary cases. Examples can intensify, clarify and encapsulate an argument, but more than that, in the best cases, examples do not act so much to complete an argument as to rupture it.

1. Water and the City

One doesn't have to like being in the water to want to live near it. Unlike my childhood friends in Manila, I was never keen on water sports; yet, to this day, I cannot imagine living far from the sea. There is something about being next to a large body of water that defines a metropolis. Of course, I'm well aware of major cities that are no less cosmopolitan for being landlocked. Sometimes a river or lake suffices—Paris and Chicago come to mind. To compare Kuala Lumpur, the city of my birth, with Singapore, where I presently reside, is, for me at any rate, to find the former somewhat more urbane, and the latter more suburban. But what K. L. lacks, by not sitting next to the Straits of Malacca, is a sense of stark horizon. Doubtless, there are exceptions: Las Vegas has a horizon effect of its own, since the desert, in many ways, can seem like an ocean. (I've always had trouble reading Los Angeles—with the Pacific on the one side and endless urban sprawl on the other.) What I'm trying to evoke is not so much the historical fact that great cities have often developed from maritime trade, but rather the archetype of the city as predicated on an edge. And water has been such a powerful visual, physical and metaphorical marker of the city's limits.

Singapore is an island city-state, not just literally but perhaps conceptually as well. Consider three stereotypical images: one, a map with a red dot, signifying a small population of mostly ethnic Chinese, surrounded by a racialized green sea of Islam; two, a teleological narrative of overcoming the odds to survive—having no hinterland or natural resources—only to suffer the pressure of striving to be competitive in an ever-changing global economy; and three, Singapore as a hub through which capital flows, without any content of its own. Much has been said that critiques and complexifies these images, anxieties and rhetorics, and I won't rehearse those arguments here. My aim is to speak less *about* than *from* Singapore.

2. These Waters; Universal Water

Given the brevity of this text, it seems a more difficult option to try to speak from a place than about it. Yet I want to try and show how a certain reflexivity about the conditions of speaking about art in general reflects the conditions of speaking about Singapore in particular. Singapore doesn't get much attention from the international art world. And when it comes to any art—local, international, contemporary or traditional—Singaporeans suffer from an attention deficit disorder of their own. The short text about art from Singapore is the discursive mode by default. Rare or endangered are lengthy discussions of the subject. Local platforms run out of steam after a few years, as they lack any sustained financial support, and the space allotted in international publications is often limited to some two thousand words.

So, I'd like to take this occasion to talk a bit about writing short texts on art. My essay title started its life as a generic vagary one would expect to change and take shape well before the completed text was submitted to the commissioning curator/editor. In this case, however, the generic-sounding phrase "water essay" seemed apt, and stuck. For what I want to talk about here is something very generic indeed: prepositions. It is my way of responding to the query that Marilu Knode

Water Essay ~~~~~~~~~~~~~~~~~~~~~~~~~ Weng-Choy Lee

alism," *Flash Art* 266 (Oct. 2002), 92.

[48] See Nicholas Van Hear, *New Diasporas: The Mass Exodus, Dispersal and Regrouping of Migrant Communities* (Seattle: University of Washington Press, 1998).

[49] Carolyn Christov-Bakargiev, in *Sabrina Mezzaqui*, exh. cat. (San Gimignano and Brescia: galleria continua and Galleria Massimo Minini, 2002), n.p.

[50] See official JSK website: http://jsk.belala.com.

[51] Ngheim Van, *Flood Myth*, 318.

[52] Thomas McCarthy, "Reconciling Unity and Diversity," in Gaonkar, *Alternative Modernities*, 213.

[53] Jung, *Man and His Symbols*, 77–78.

screen (monitor) to play video taken from automobile.

度的 ● **PDP** or LCD or 电视 (一定是高亮度) 播放

screen.

ection.

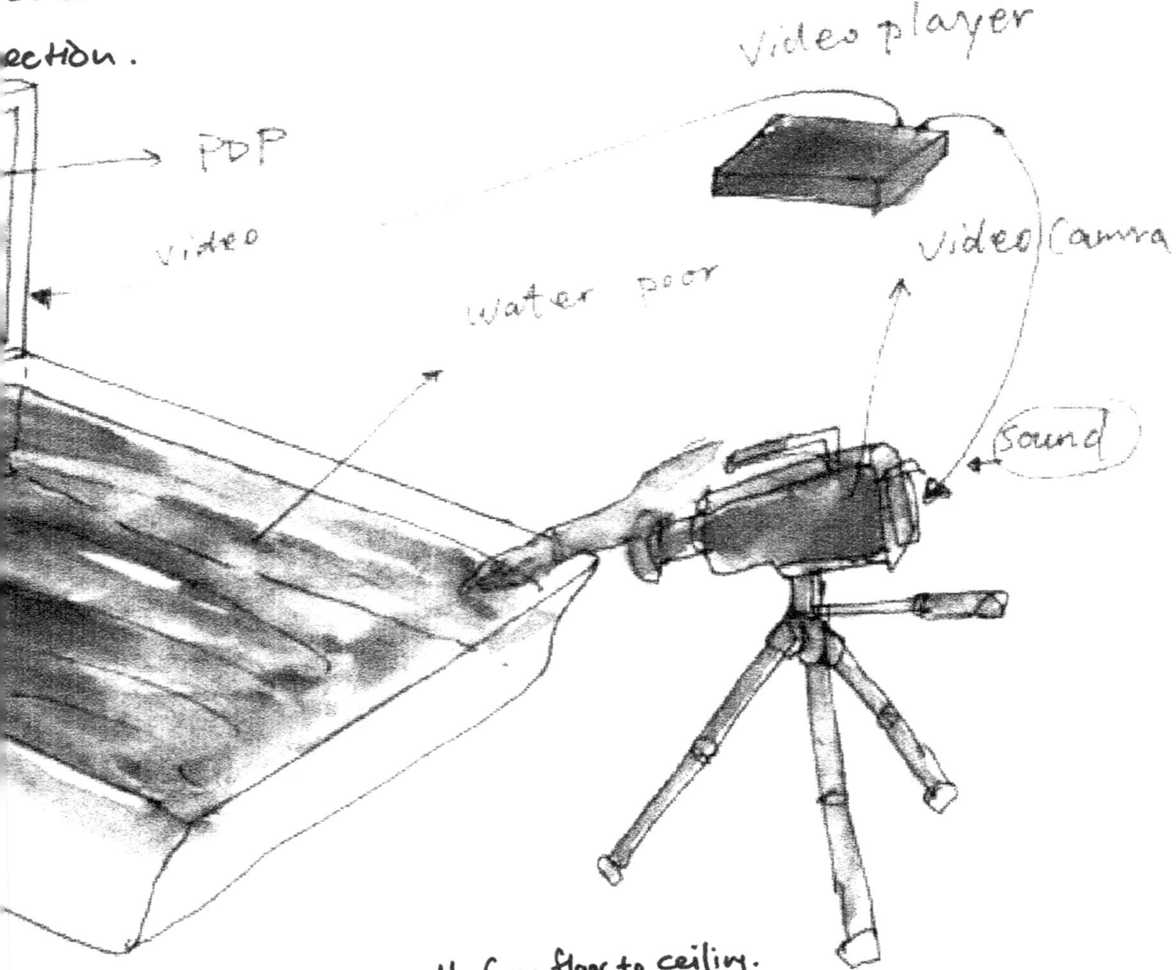

→ PDP

video

water poor

video player

video camra

sound

ge). size according to wall, from floor to ceiling.

的作品自有" 方法更们) 尺顶天立地 (尽量大) Bigger is Better.

(三) 人员帮助. 3. Assistance:

① 翻译一名. ① translator

② 助手一名. 他可以操作机器和摄镜.

② Assistant who knows how to use video equipment.

jector (2).

Requires a <u>high-resolution</u>, <u>bright</u> PDP or LC[

③ 将 摄好 的 video 在 大屏幕 高解[

large container of water to reflect th[

④ 用 水盆 反射

Use a video camera to record the r[

⑤ 用 摄像机 捕摄 水的 反射

His hand will continuously

手在不断地敲击

tap the water so

画面中的影物

the image reflected

使水面影像变化

will be disrupted.

被打碎

1. Needed Equipment:

一. 所需设备 (拍摄作品用)

① Hi-resolution video camera.
① 高清晰度 摄像机 一台

② Hi-resolution video player.
② 高清晰度 播放机 一台

③ high resolution, bright PDP or LCD monitor.
③ 高清晰 高亮度 的 大屏幕 电子显示屏

④ Large water container
④ 大水盆 一个

⑤ Hi-resolution video tapes (6).
⑤ 高清晰 录像带 6 盘

⑥ ink.

2. Exhibition equipment:
二. 展出设备 ① Display screen. (see details first.
① 展示用幕 (与声称清 Chambers Fine Art 中的

② video project x2 高清晰度 高亮度 大投影[
② Hi resolution, bright, large [

③ DVD player x2

④ speakers x 2

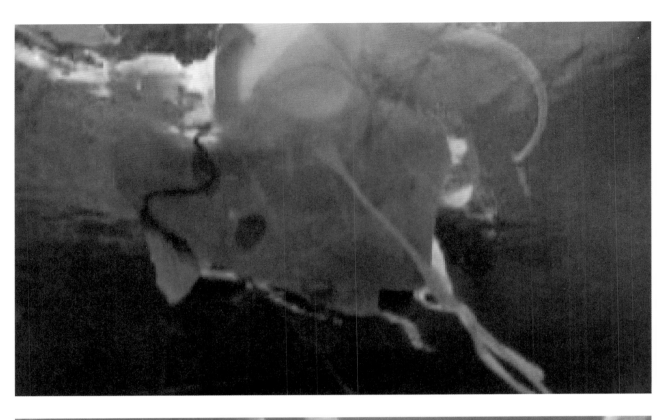

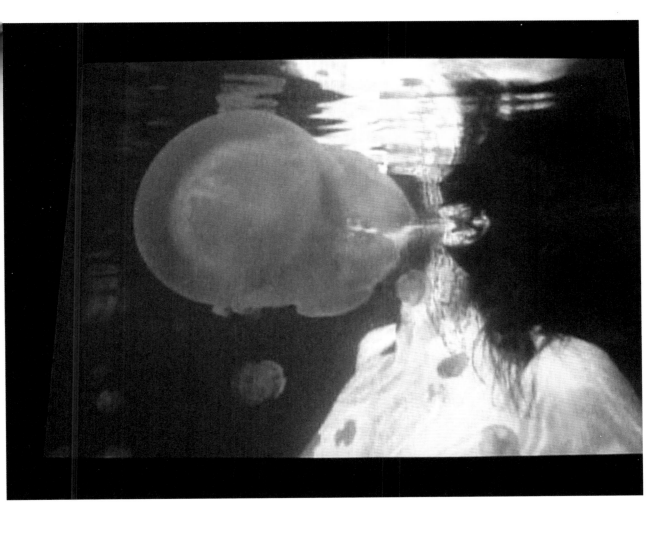

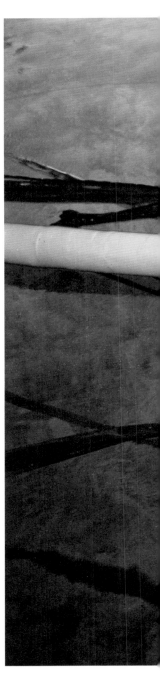

Janaina Tschäpe
stills from *Blood, Sea*

2004

Stan Douglas
stills from *Nutka·*

1996

installation view, *Reality Film*, 2001

detail, drawing for *Mother of the World #2*

painter Mahmoud Masry

Lara Baladi

detail, *Mother of the World #2* **2005**

Lara Baladi
installation view, *Mother of the World #2*
2005

Dorothy Cross
still from *Teacup*
1997

Dorothy Cross

still from *Jellyfish Lake*

2002

Checklist of the Exhibition

1. Lara Baladi
Mother of theWorld #2 [Oum el Dounia], 2005
hand-painted billboard
painted by Mahmoud El Masry and Mustapa El Faky
78 x 218 inches
Produced by the Scottsdale Museum of Contemporary Art
with funding from The Andy Warhol Foundation for the
Visual Arts, Inc., New York
Courtesy of the artist, Cairo

2. Dorothy Cross
Teacup, 1997
single-channel video
running time 3 minutes
Collection Rebecca and Alexander Stewart, Seattle

3. Dorothy Cross
Jellyfish Lake, 2002
single-channel video projection
running time 6 minutes
Courtesy of the artist and Kerlin Gallery, Dublin

4. Jacci Den Hartog
Dream of the Blue Chamber, 2004
polyurethane and steel
48½ x 103¼ x 44 inches
Courtesy of the artist and Christopher Grimes Gallery,
Los Angeles

5. Jacci Den Hartog
Part of the Tide, 2004
polyurethane and steel
2 x 252 x 10 inches
Collection of Jones Day, Los Angeles

6. Stan Douglas
Nu•tka•, 1996
single-channel video projection with audio
running time 6:50 minutes
216 x 336 inches
Courtesy of the artist and David Zwirner Gallery, New York

7. Tony Feher
How to MakeWaterWetter, 2005
mixed media
12 x 24 x 6 inches
Produced by the Scottsdale Museum of Contemporary Art
with funding from The Andy Warhol Foundation for the
Visual Arts, Inc., New York
Courtesy of the artist and D'Amelio Terras, New York

8. Tony Feher
It Has Something to Do with Trickle Down, 2005
mixed media
dimensions variable
Produced by the Scottsdale Museum of Contemporary Art
with funding from The Andy Warhol Foundation for the
Visual Arts, Inc., New York
Courtesy of the artist and D'Amelio Terras, New York

9. Robert Gober
Untitled, 1998–2004
cast pewter, AP 2/2, ed. 8
3¾ x 1¼ inches
Courtesy of the artist and Matthew Marks Gallery, New York

10. Robert Gober
Untitled, 1998–2004
silver-plated bronze, resin and paint
66½ x 7¾ x 2¼ inches
Courtesy of the artist and Matthew Marks Gallery, New York

11. Laura Horelli
Helsinki Shipyard/Port San Juan, 2002–03
two-channel video
running time *Helsinki Shipyard* 14:18 minutes
running time *Port San Juan* 17:37 minutes
Produced with the support of PR'02 [En Ruta], M&M
Proyectos, Paula Toppila, FRAME and City of Helsinki

Artists' Biographies

LARA BALADI
Lara Baladi was born in Beirut, Lebanon, in 1969. She studied at Richmond University, London. She lives and works in Cairo.

SOLO EXHIBITIONS 2004: *Kai'ro*, BildMuseet, Umeå Universitet, Sweden; with travel to Björneborgs Konstmuseum, Finland; Nikolaj Københavns Kommunes Udstillingsbygning, Copenhagen; and Länsmuseet Västernorrland, Härnösand, Sweden. 2002: *Al Fanous al Sehry*, Townhouse Gallery of Contemporary Art, Cairo. 2001: *Sandouk El Dounia*, Ashkal Alwan, Beirut.

GROUP EXHIBITIONS 2004: *Afrika Remix: Contemporary Art of a Continent*, Kunst Palast, Düsseldorf; with travel to Hayward Gallery, London; Centre Georges Pompidou, Paris; and Mori Art Museum, Tokyo; *3èmes Rencontres de la Photographie*, Bamako, Mali. 2003: *DisORIENTation: Contemporary Arab Art from the Middle East*, Haus der Kulturen der Welt, Berlin; *Zakrayat, Cairo Modern Art in Holland*, Stage Holding, The Hague, Netherlands.
==

DOROTHY CROSS
Dorothy Cross was born in Cork, Ireland, in 1956. She studied at Crawford Municipal School of Art, Cork, 1973–74; Leicester Polytechnic, England, 1974–77; and received an MFA from the San Francisco Art Institute in 1982. She lives and works in Dublin.

SOLO EXHIBITIONS 2003: *H2O*, Elaine L. Jacob Gallery, Wayne State University, Detroit; with travel to Western Gallery, Western Washington University, Bellingham. 2002: *GTECH/ NO/ ZONE*, Museum of Contemporary Art, Taipei; *Salve*, Kerlin Gallery, Dublin. 2001: *Come into the Garden Maude* and *Fourth Wall*, commissions for Public Art Development Trust, London, for the National Theatre, London.

GROUP EXHIBITIONS 2004: *Public and Private Narratives*, Irish Museum of Modern Art, Dublin. 2003: *Liquid Sea*, Museum of Contemporary Art, Sydney. 2002: *In the Freud Museum*, Freud Museum, London; *Aquaria*, Oberosterreichische Landesgalerie, Linz; with travel to Städtische Kunstsammlungen, Chemnitz; Museo d'Arte Moderna, Bologna; and Charlottenborg Udstillingsbygning, Copenhagen.
==

JACCI DEN HARTOG
Jacci Den Hartog was born in Pella, Iowa, in 1962. She studied at Centro Cultural Costarricense Norteamericano, San José, Costa Rica, in 1982; received a BA in fine art in 1984 from Linfield College, McMinnville, Oregon, and an MFA in sculpture in 1986 from Claremont Graduate School, California. She lives and works in Los Angeles.

SOLO EXHIBITIONS 2004: *Moonshine*, Christopher Grimes Gallery, Santa Monica. 2000: Contemporary Arts Center, Cincinnati, Ohio. 1998: San Francisco Art Institute. 1995: White Columns, New York.

GROUP EXHIBITIONS 2003–04: *UnNaturally*, organized by Independent Curators International, with travel to Long Beach Museum of Art, California; University of South Florida, Contemporary Art Museum, Tampa; Kansas City Art Institute, Missouri; Fisher Gallery, UCLA, Los Angeles; Copia: The American Center for Wine, Food and the Arts, Napa, California; and Lowe Art Museum, University of Miami, Coral Gables. 2002: *Representing Landscape*, University Art Gallery, University of California, San Diego.
==

STAN DOUGLAS
Stan Douglas was born in Vancouver, Canada, in 1960. He graduated from the Emily Carr College of Art, Vancouver, in 1982. He lives and works in Vancouver.

SOLO EXHIBITIONS 2005: *Stan Douglas: Inconsolable Memories*, Joslyn Art Museum, Omaha. 2004: *Cuba*, David Zwirner, New York. 2003: *Stan Douglas: Film Installations and Photographs*, Kestnergesellschaft, Hannover, Germany. 2002: *Journey into Fear*, Contemporary Art Gallery, Vancouver. 2001: *Le Détroit*, Kunsthalle Basel; Winnipeg

Cultural and Library Committee
Courtesy of the artist and Galerie Barbara Weiss, Berlin

12. Roni Horn
three *Untitled* from the series *Still Water (The River Thames, for Example)*, 1999
offset lithographs
30½ x 41½ inches each
Courtesy of the artist and Matthew Marks Gallery, New York

13. Ange Leccia
The Sea [La Mer], 2001
single-channel video projection
running time 60 minutes
Courtesy of the artist and Galerie Almine Rech, Paris

14. Sabrina Mezzaqui
A Thousand and One Nights—Radio Tunisia [Le mille e una notte—Radio Tunisi], 1998
single-channel video with audio
running time 3:10 minutes
Courtesy of the artist and galleria continua, San Gimigniano, Italy

15. Rivane Neuenschwander
Belong, Not Belong, 2000
nine incorporated color coupler prints, laminated on aluminum
35½ x 27½ inches each
Collection Linda Pace, San Antonio, Texas

16. Rivane Neuenschwander
Love Lettering, 2002
single-channel video with audio
running time 6:30 minutes
Collection Linda Pace, San Antonio, Texas

17. Jun Nguyen-Hatsushiba
Memorial Project, Nha Trang, Vietnam—Towards the Complex—For the Courageous, the Curious and the Cowards, 2001
single-channel video projection with audio
running time 13 minutes
Courtesy of the artist and Lehmann Maupin Gallery, New York

18. Song Dong
Floating: Scottsdale, 2005
two-channel video projection
running time right 21:38 minutes
running time left 17:16 minutes
72 x 192 inches
Produced by the Scottsdale Museum of Contemporary Art with funding from The Andy Warhol Foundation for the Visual Arts, Inc., New York
Courtesy of the artist and Chambers Fine Arts, New York

19. Janaina Tschäpe
Blood, Sea, 2004
four-channel video projection with audio
running time 13:48 minutes
Originally commissioned by the University of South Florida Contemporary Art Museum for the exhibition *Janaina Tschäpe: Blood, Sea*
Courtesy of the artist and Brent Sikkema Gallery, New York

20. Carrie Yamaoka
Koolpop #18, 2004
mylar, flexible urethane resin and mixed media
46½ x 39½ inches
Courtesy of the artist, New York

21. Carrie Yamaoka
68 by 12 (blue.green), 2005
mylar, flexible urethane resin and mixed media
49½ x 20¾ x 12 inches
Private collection, Scottsdale

Art Gallery; and Hamburger Bahnhof–Museum für Gegenwart, Berlin. 2000: *Le Détroit*, Art Institute of Chicago. 1999: *Stan Douglas*, Vancouver Art Gallery; with travel to Edmonton Art Gallery; The Power Plant, Toronto; De Pont Museum, Tilburg, Netherlands; and Museum of Contemporary Art, Los Angeles; *Le Détroit*, Art Gallery of Windsor.

GROUP EXHIBITIONS 2004: *Perspectives @ 25: A Quarter Century of New Art in Houston*, Contemporary Arts Museum, Houston; *Baja to Vancouver: The West Coast and Contemporary Art*, organized by and traveling to Seattle Art Museum; Museum of Contemporary Art, San Diego; Vancouver Art Gallery; and CCA Wattis Institute, San Francisco; *Friedrich Christian Flick Collection*, Hamburger Bahnhof–Museum für Gegenwart, Berlin; *Prefix Photo*, Prefix Institute of Contemporary Art, Toronto; *Videodreams: Between the Cinematic and the Theatrical*, Kunsthaus Graz, Austria; "*We Come In Peace*"/*Histories of the Americas*, Musée d'Art Contemporain de Montréal; *Thriller*, Edmonton Art Gallery; *Techniques of the Visible*, Shanghai Biennale, China; *Éblouissement*, Jeu de Paume, Paris.

===

TONY FEHER

Tony Feher was born in Albuquerque, New Mexico, in 1956. He received a BA from the University of Texas, Austin. He lives and works in New York.

SOLO EXHIBITIONS 2004: La Fundación "la Caixa," Lleida, Spain; *The Wart on the Bosom of Mother Nature*, D'Amelio Terras, New York. 2002: Tony Feher, *Matrix 201a: I'm Tired of Toast*, Berkeley Art Museum; *Tony Feher: Maybe/Enjoy*, Worcester Art Museum. 2001: *The Red Room and More*, Center for Curatorial Studies, Bard College, Annandale-on-Hudson, New York; *The Red Room and More*, UCLA Hammer Museum, Los Angeles.

GROUP EXHIBITIONS 2004: *Bottle: Contemporary Art and Vernacular Tradition*, The Aldrich Contemporary Art Museum, Ridgefield, Connecticut; *The Reality of Things*, Triple Candie, New York; *How Sculptors See*, Worcester Art Museum, Massachusetts; Project Room 4: *Where Love and Time Collide*, Centraal Museum, Utrecht, Netherlands; *State of Play*, Serpentine Gallery, London.

===

ROBERT GOBER

Robert Gober was born in Wallingford, Connecticut, in 1954. He studied at Middlebury College, Vermont, and the Tyler School of Art, Temple University, Elkins Park, Pennsylvania. He lives and works in New York.

SOLO EXHIBITIONS 2005: Matthew Marks Gallery, New York. 2003: *Robert Gober Displacements*, Astrup Fearnley Museet for Moderne Kunst, Oslo. 2001: XLIX Biennale di Venezia, Venice; Museum für Gegenwartskunst, Basel. 1999: *Robert Gober: Sculpture + Drawing*, Walker Art Center, Minneapolis; with travel to Rooseum, Malmö, Sweden; Hirshhorn Museum and Sculpture Garden, Smithsonian Institution, Washington, D.C.; and San Francisco Museum of Modern Art. 1998: *Robert Gober*, The Aldrich Contemporary Art Museum, Ridgefield, Connecticut. 1997: *Robert Gober*, Museum of Contemporary Art, Los Angeles.

GROUP EXHIBITIONS 2004: *Das Große Fressen. Von Pop bis heute*, Kunsthalle Bielefeld, Germany; *Repulsion*, University Galleries, College of Fine Arts, Illinois State University, Normal; *Singular Forms (Sometimes Repeated): Art from 1951 to the Present*, Solomon R. Guggenheim Museum, New York; *Bodily Space–New Obsessions in Figurative Sculpture*, Albright-Knox Art Gallery, Buffalo; *The Reality of Things*, Triple Candie, New York; *Off the Wall: Works from the JPMorgan Chase Collection*, Bruce Museum, Greenwich, Connecticut; *Open*, Arcadia University Art Gallery, Glenside, Pennsylvania; *Monument to Now*, DESTE Foundation–Center for Contemporary Art, Athens; *Between Art and Life: The Contemporary Painting and Sculpture Collection*, San Francisco Museum of Modern Art; SITE Santa Fe, New Mexico; *Mirrorical Returns: Marcel Duchamp and 20th Century Art*, The National Museum of Art in Osaka, Japan; with travel to Yokohama Museum, Japan.

===

RONI HORN

Roni Horn was born in New York in 1955. She received a BFA from Rhode Island School of Design in 1975 and an MFA from Yale University in 1978. She lives and works in New York.

SOLO EXHIBITIONS   2004: *Roni Horn. In der Sammlung*, Museum Folkwang, Essen; *Some Thames*, Art Institute of Chicago. 2003: *If on a Winter's Night . . . Roni Horn . . .*, Fotomuseum Winterthur, Zurich; *Roni Horn*, Centre Georges Pompidou, Paris; with travel to Fondazione Bevilacqua La Masa, Venice. 2002: *Clowndoubt*, Matthew Marks Gallery, New York.

GROUP EXHIBITIONS 2004: Biennial Exhibition, Whitney Museum of American Art, New York; *Paisaje y Memoria*, La Casa Encendida, Madrid; with travel to Centro Atlántico de Arte Moderno (CAAM), Canary Islands, Spain; *Drawing Modern: Works from the Agnes Gund Collection*, Cleveland Museum of Art, Ohio; *Capp Street Project: 20th Anniversary Exhibition*, CCA Wattis Institute for Contemporary Art, San Francisco. 2003: *Contemporary Photography from the Harn Museum Collection (Part I)*, Samuel P. Harn Museum of Art, University of South Florida, Gainesville.

==

ANGE LECCIA

Ange Leccia was born in Minervu, Corsica, in 1952. He studied at the Université Paris, Pantheon–Sorbonne, 1972–76. He lives and works in Paris.

SOLO EXHIBITIONS   2005: *Ange Leccia*, Musée National Picasso La Guerre et la Paix, Vallauris, France; *Ange Leccia—La Mer*, Musée d'Art Moderne de la Ville de Paris. 2004: Festival Rayon Frais, Château de Tours, France. 2003: *Avant Travaux*, École d'Architecture, Versailles; Galerie Almine Rech, Paris. 2002: *Christophe* (in collaboration with Dominique Gonzalez-Foerster), Palais de Tokyo, Paris. 2001: *Les eléments*, Musée Fesch, Ajaccio, France.

GROUP EXHIBITIONS 2004: *Intra-Muros*, Musée d'Art Moderne et d'Art Contemporain, Nice, France; *Contrepoint. L'Art contemporain au Louvre*, Musée du Louvre, Paris. 2003: *L'Invention du monde*, Centre Georges Pompidou, Paris.

==

SABRINA MEZZAQUI

Sabrina Mezzaqui was born in Bologna, Italy, in 1964. In 1985 she received a degree from the Istituto Statale d'Arte, Bologna, and graduated from the Accademia di Belle Arti, also in Bologna, in 1993. She lives and works in Marzabotto, Italy.

SOLO EXHIBITIONS   2002: *Le mille e una notte (Radio Tunisi)*, Institute of Visual Arts *(inova)*, University of Wisconsin-Milwaukee; *Vocabolario*, Viafarini, Milan. 2001: *Carezze*, galleria continua, San Gimignano, Italy. 2000: *Pensieri in sottofondo*, Palazzo Tozzoni, Imola, Italy.

GROUP EXHIBITIONS 2004: *Settlements*, Musée d'Art Moderne Saint-Étienne Métropole, France. 2003: *Moltitudini-Solitudini*, Museo d'Arte Moderna e Contemporanea, Bologna; *Il palazzo delle libertà*, Palazzo delle Papesse–Centro Arte Contemporanea, Siena; *Del segno del suono e della parola*, Progetto Arti Visive, Berchidda, Italy; *Il nuovo ritratto d'Europa*, Académie Royale de Belgique, Brussels; *Assenze/Presenze*, Le Botanique, Brussels.

==

RIVANE NEUENSCHWANDER

Rivane Neuenschwander was born in Belo Horizonte, Brazil, in 1967. She received a BA in fine art from Federal University, Minas Gerais, Brazil, in 1993, and an MA from the Royal College of Art, London, in 1998. She lives and works in Belo Horizonte, Brazil.

SOLO EXHIBITIONS   2005: *Currents 93: Rivane Neuenschwander*, St. Louis Art Museum. 2003: *Superficial Resemblance*, Palais de Tokyo, Paris. 2002: *Rivane Neuenschwander. Olhara Poeira, Por Exemplo*, Museu de Arte Moderna Aloísio Magalhães, Recife, Brazil; *To/From: Rivane Neuenschwander*, Walker Art Center, Minneapolis. 2000: Galeria Fortes Vilaça, São Paulo.

GROUP EXHIBITIONS 2005: *Urban Cocktail*, Walker Art Center, Minneapolis. 2004: *Cinema e Arte*, Culturgest, Lisbon, Portugal; *New Acquisitions 2003–Collection Gilberto Chateaubriand*, Museu de Arte Moderna, Rio de Janeiro; *Brazil: Body Nostalgia*, The National Museum of Modern Art, Tokyo; with travel to The National Museum of Modern Art, Kyoto; *(Dys)Function*, Kunsthall, Lund, Switzerland.
===

JUN NGUYEN-HATSUSHIBA

Jun Nguyen-Hatsushiba was born in Tokyo in 1968. He studied at Brookhaven College, Dallas, received a BFA from the School of the Art Institute of Chicago in 1992 and an MFA from Maryland Institute College of Art, Mount Royal School of Art, Baltimore, in 1994. He lives and works in Ho Chi Minh City, Vietnam.

SOLO EXHIBITIONS 2004: Lehmann Maupin, New York; *MAM Project 002: Jun Nguyen-Hatsushiba*, Mori Art Museum, Tokyo; *Memorial Project Vietnam*, Centro Atlántico de Arte Moderno (CAAM), Canary Islands, Spain.

GROUP EXHIBITIONS 2004: *Encounters in the 21st Century*, 21st Century Museum of Contemporary Art, Kanazawa, Japan; Seville Biennale, Seville; Shanghai Biennale, Shanghai Art Museum; *Movimento/Movimenti*, Villa Cattolica, Bagheria, Italy; *At the Still Point of the Turning World*, FACT Centre, Liverpool; *Vis Vitalis*, Centraal Museum, Utrecht, Netherlands; *Artes Mundi Exhibition*, National Museum and Gallery, Cardiff, Wales; *Material Witness*, Museum of Contemporary Art, Cleveland, Ohio.
===

SONG DONG

Song Dong was born in Beijing, China, in 1966. He graduated from the Department of Fine Art, Capital Normal University, Beijing, in 1989. He lives and works in Beijing.

SOLO EXHIBITIONS 2002: *Chopsticks*, Chambers Fine Art, New York. 2000: *Song Dong in London*, The Tablet Gallery, London. 1999: *Jump*, Tian An Men, Beijing; *Temporary Office Construction*, Tao Gallery, Beijing; *Slap*, Ruine for Arts, Berlin; *158 Stone (1840–1997)*, Schezhen, China. 1997: *Look*, Contemporary Art Museum, Beijing.

GROUP EXHIBITIONS 2004: XXVI Bienal Internacional de São Paulo, Brazil; *Slow Rushes*, Contemporary Art Centre, Vilnius, Lithuania; *Summer Breeze*, Art Beatus Exchange Square, Hong Kong; *The Logbook—An Art-Project about Communication and Cultural Exchange*, Long March Foundation, Beijing; *Is It Art?*, Noanoa Center and Shanxi Provincial Art Museum, Xian, China; *Asian Traffic*, Asia-Australia Arts Centre, Sydney; *Doing Nothing Anywhere Is*, Vitamin Creative Space, Guangzhou, China; *Concrete Horizons: Contemporary Art from China*, Adam Art Gallery, Wellington, New Zealand; *Between Past and Future: New Photography and Video from China*, organized by International Center of Photography, New York, and David and Alfred Smart Museum of Art, Chicago; with travel to Seattle Art Museum; Museum of Contemporary Art, Chicago; Haus der Kulturen der Welt, Berlin; and Santa Barbara Museum of Art.
===

JANAINA TSCHÄPE

Janaina Tschäpe was born in Munich, Germany, in 1973. She studied art at the Hochschule für Bildende Kunst, Hamburg, Germany, and received an MFA in 1998 from the School of Visual Arts, New York. She lives and works in New York and Rio de Janeiro, Brazil.

SOLO EXHIBITIONS 2004: *The Sea and The Mountain*, Brent Sikkema Gallery, New York; *Blood, Sea*, University of South Florida, Contemporary Art Museum, Tampa. 2003: *Agua Viva*, Nichido Contemporary Art, Tokyo; *The Moat and the Moon*, Images au Centre, Le Château d'Azay-le-Rideau, France.

GROUP EXHIBITIONS 2005: *ACTING OUT: Invented Melodrama in Contemporary Photography*, University of Iowa Museum of Art, Iowa City. 2004: *Experimental Cinema*, Centre Georges Pompidou, Paris; *Landscape Confection*, Wexner Center for the Arts, Ohio State University, Columbus; *Order and Chaos*, Fotomuseum Winterthur, Zurich.
===

CARRIE YAMAOKA

Carrie Yamaoka was born in 1957 in Glen Cove, New York. She attended the Tyler School of Art, Rome, 1977–78, and received a BA from Wesleyan University, Middletown, Connecticut, in 1979. She lives and works in New York.

SOLO EXHIBITIONS   2005: *Portholes, Potholes and Portals*, Galerie Une, Neuchâtel, Switzerland. 2004: *world hotel*, Debs & Co., New York; *New York: Carrie Yamaoka*, Studio 1.1, London; *Carrie Yamaoka: Recent Work*, Aeroplastics Contemporary, Brussels.

GROUP EXHIBITIONS   2005: *Extreme Abstraction*, Albright-Knox Art Gallery, Buffalo; *Vanishing Point*, Wexner Center for the Arts, Ohio State University, Columbus; *Surfaces Paradise*, Museum voor Moderne Kunst, Arnhem, Netherlands. 2004: *Live Forever, or Die Trying (Manic Abstract Painting Now)*, Torch Gallery, Amsterdam. 2003: *Without Fear or Reproach: Pulse of America*, Aeroplastics Contemporary and Witte Zaal, Ghent, Belgium. 2002: *Mirror Mirror*, MASS MoCA, North Adams, Massachusetts; *Painting as Paradox*, Artists Space, New York; *Portrait Obscured*, San Jose Institute of Contemporary Art.
===

Tony Feher

How to Make Water Wetter

2005

Jacci Den Hartog
Dream of the Blue Chamber   **2004**

Jacci Den Hartog

Part of the Tide
detail *Part of the Tide*

2004

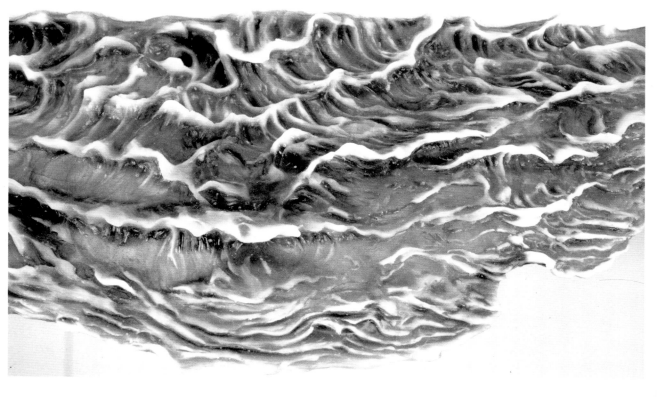

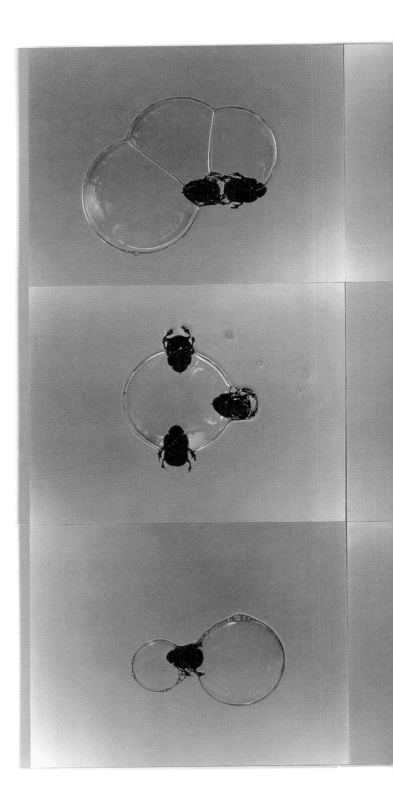

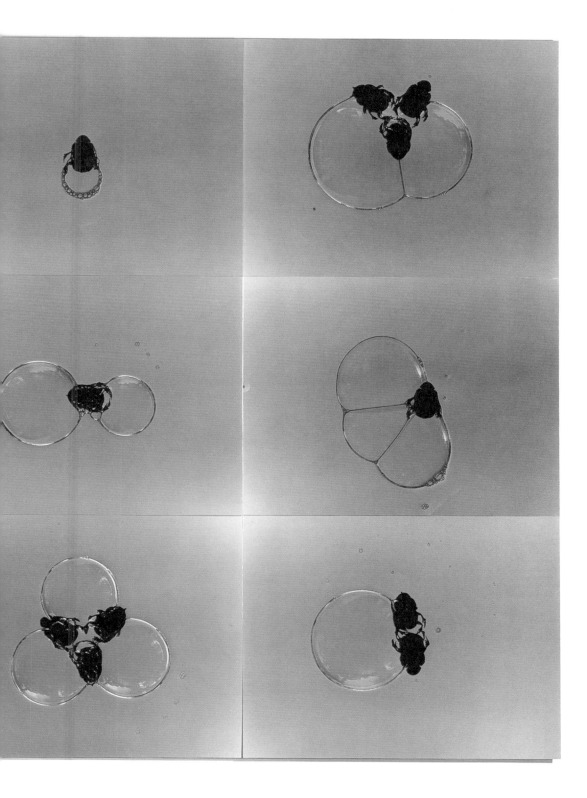

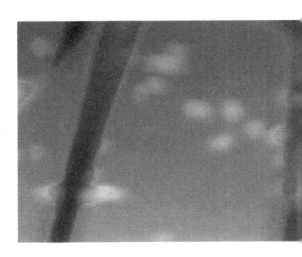

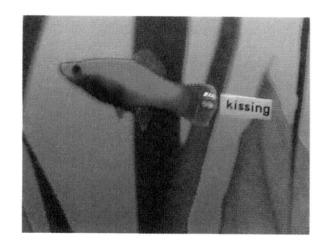

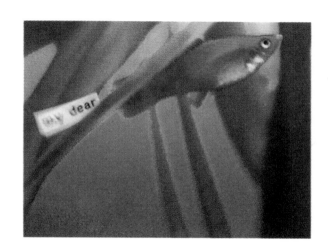

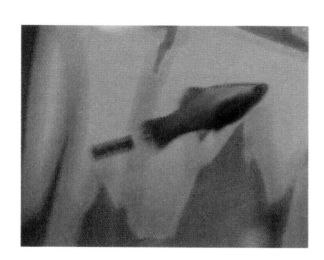

Sabrina Mezzaqui
still from *A Thousand and One Nights–Radio Tunisia*
1998

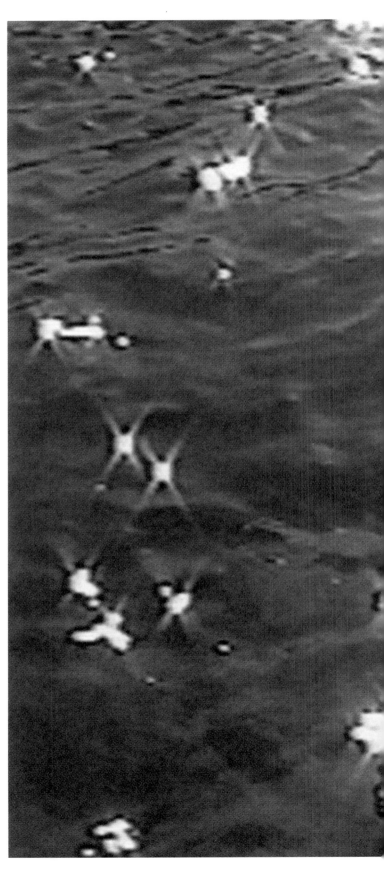

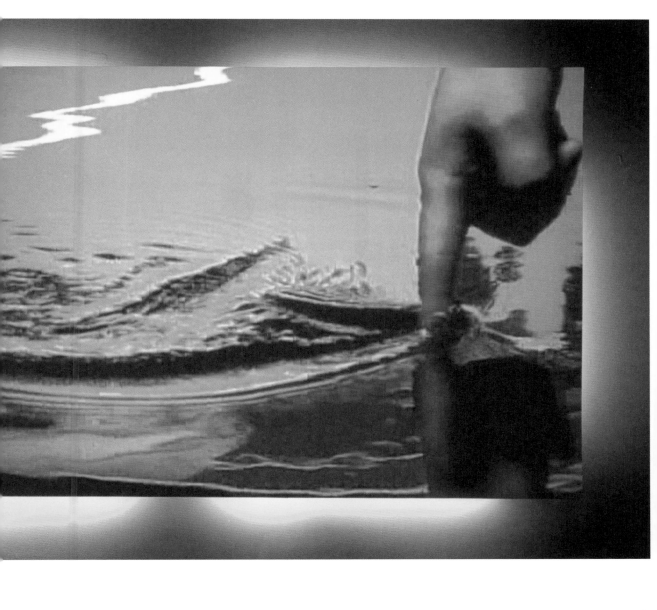

Yes, these ships are already cities.

Laura Horelli

stills from *Helsinki Shipyard / Port San Juan*
detail *Helsinki*   **2002–03**

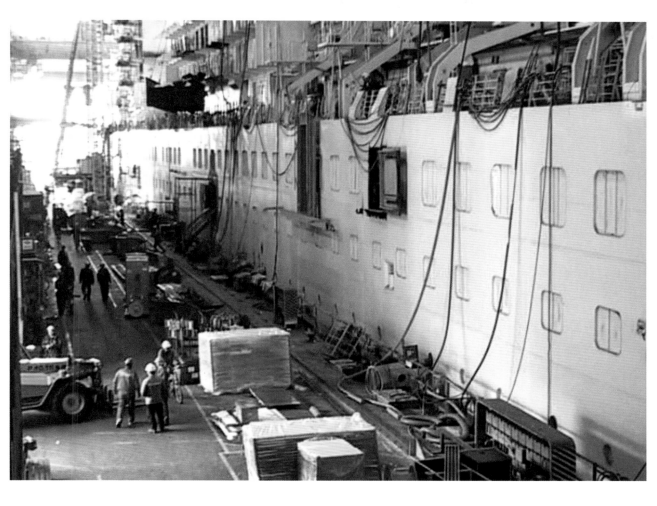

Laura Horelli

stills from *Helsinki Shipyard / Port San Juan*
detail *San Juan*

2002–03

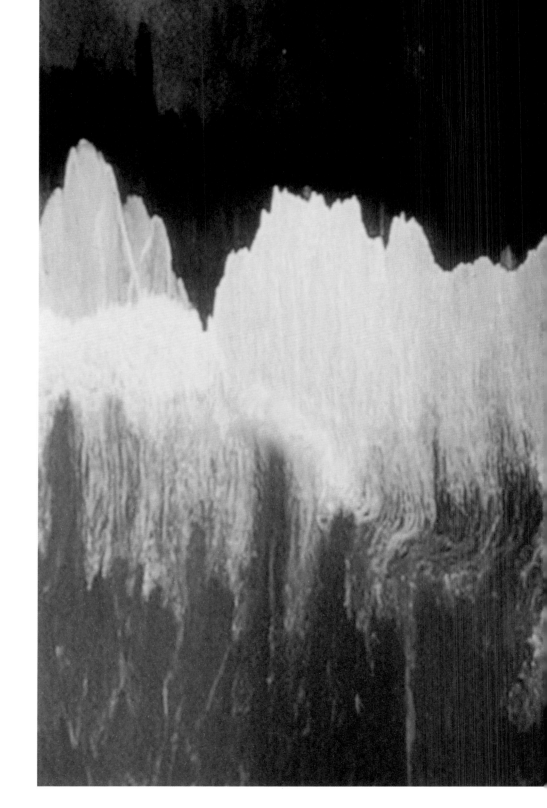

Ange Leccia still from *The Sea* 2001

Roni Horn

Untitled from the series Still Water (The River Thames, for Example)
1999

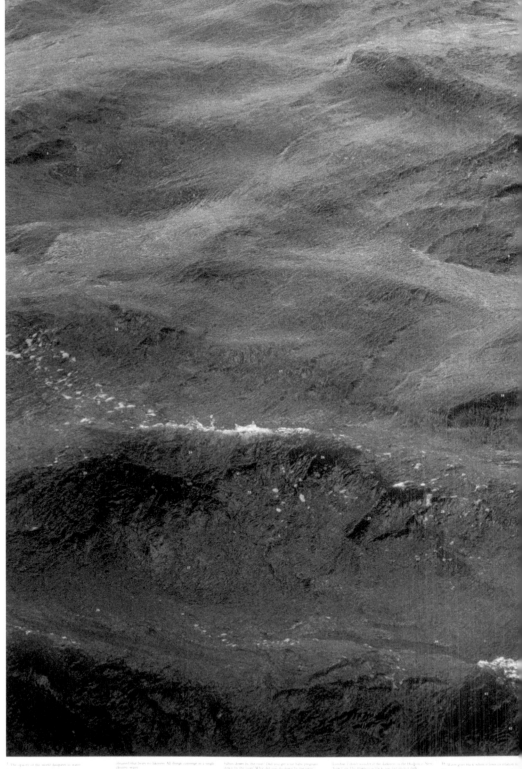

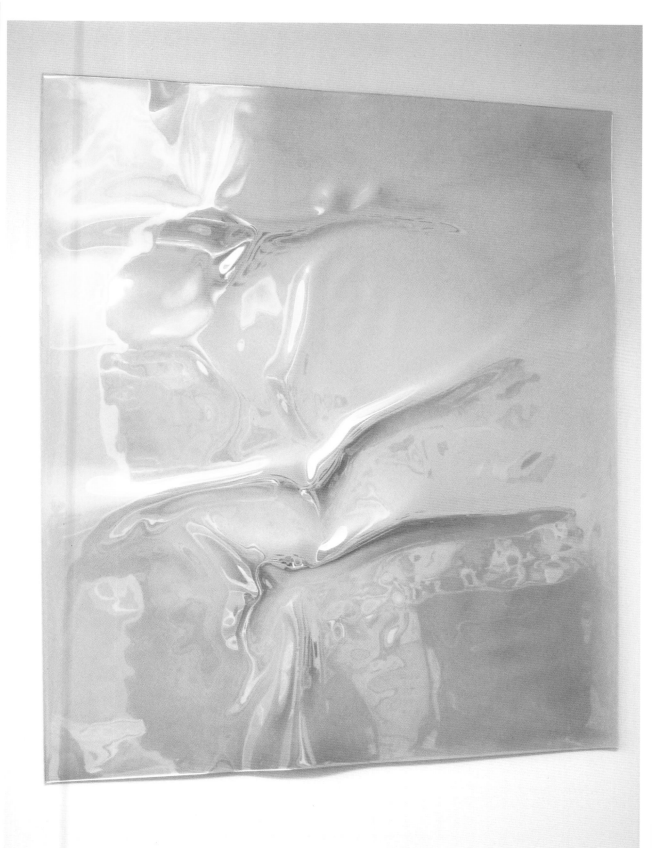

Carrie Yamaoka

68 by 12 (blue green)

2005

Robert Gober

Untitled

1998–2004

Robert Gober

detail of *Untitled*

1998–2004

Tony Feher

detail of *It Has Something to Do with Trickle Down*

2005

Tony Feher

detail of *It Has Something to Do with Trickle Down*
2005